Doors
of
Light

The Awakening Has Begun

My niece Thaherha,

Love you to the moon!! ;)

Best Wishes :)

Love,

Trenage

Dedication

I dedicate this book to my loving family. Starting with my father, Sir. Charles R. Talbert, for without him I would not be the woman I am today. To my mother, Velma Brown, for giving me life. To my children, Sumayyah, Najada, Javier, and my grandson Makai, for bringing so much love and joy into my life. And to my uncle, Sir. Rallie Talbert Jr., for all the long philosophical talks and for just being the best uncle a girl could ever ask for. I love you all.

Acknowledgments

Special thanks to Marilyn Sadler, for being such a wonderful friend and for inspiring me to write this book. Thank you for all your loving support and kindness.

Doors of Light

of

The Awakening Has Begun

Trenayce Talbert

Doors of Light
The Awakening Has Begun

First published in 2015 by
Panoma Press Ltd
48 St Vincent Drive, St Albans, Herts, AL1 5SJ UK

info@panomapress.com
www.panomapress.com

Cover design by Michael Inns
Artwork by Karen Gladwell

ISBN 978-1-784520-72-4

A CIP catalogue record for this book is available from the British Library.

This book is available online and in all good bookstores.

Contents

To The Reader

At a very young age, around five or six, I was aware that I was communicating with something or someone. What, I never thought about because it came so naturally. It seemed to have been there, just as my siblings, from the time I can remember.

At that age, your imagination is strong and active, but for me, I knew it was not of my making. It clearly taught me things that a normal six-year-old would not know. It guided me. It gave me wisdom that I happily imparted to my family and friends. My mother was often one who I offered much advice to, and she would ask me where I got my information. I would simply tell her that I just knew. She says I said things that were far beyond my years and that I saved her life more than once.

The dialogue between me and this unknown voice took place in my head. It was like having an "internal parent." Whenever I was ready to involve myself in mischievous matters, the voice would tell me that I knew better and I would be risking a spanking if caught. Even at times when I knew there would be little chance of being caught – taking an extra cookie, using my sister's crayons, or even riding my sister's bike without permission – the voice would advise against it and counsel me to better judgment.

These interactions took place in other ways as well. I was able to ask simple yes or no questions and immediately receive an answer. My answers were given to me in a feeling. I would feel bad if it was no, and a sense of peace meant yes. It was this way for a very long time. Things did not change until I was around 19 years old. At that time in my life, things became more complicated. I was not able to just ask what I should do, I started being given a choice. This was completely strange to me. I wasn't used to this way of communicating. The voice would say, "Do you want to do that?" I felt like a fish out of water. I was being told that I could choose and my choices weren't so easy to make any longer. I still got feelings, but it seemed that I had more control over the outcome than before. Spirit was guiding me to a new way of communicating and interpreting, a way that not only said yes or no, but much more.

Early in my life, I would know that someone was "bad news" and that was about it. Later on, I began to be shown some of the details that made that person "bad." Details began to emerge right before my eyes. Sometimes, I would tell my mother that her new boyfriend was no good and that he was bad for her. I knew that he was not being honest and I would tell my mother to get rid of him. She always gave me a look; I could tell that it unnerved her. More than once, she came back and told me that I was right, and she always wondered how I knew. I never could give her an answer, because I didn't understand myself.

As time went on, communication with this inner voice became more like a conversation. I still can't tell you why or how it works, it just does. And the more I learned to trust it, the stronger it became. This voice continues to guide me through my life, from the very mundane to the most challenging. It has never been wrong. I may have interpreted something out of context, but after the fact, I saw where I misunderstood the message. This is the trickiest part. It's a work in progress. It's like learning a new language, one that is not spoken, but felt. This unspoken language then has to be put into our human language, which is limited by vocabulary. This task can be great. It's not the perfect translation ever, because words fall short of the total "feeling." As time has passed, I have learned to interpret more, like a child that grows in vocabulary and begins to speak in more complex ways.

The messages I receive not only concern my personal life, but I can see into others' lives as well. For a very long time, this disturbed me. I did not know how to shut it off. I couldn't enjoy the simplest of things, like going to the library or grocery shopping. A fleeting glance in the direction of someone was all it took for me to know some pretty personal details about them. I finally learned how to turn this off, at least most of the time, but sometimes it's completely out of my control. It took me years to be able to go to the mall or to the grocery store when it was crowded, because I used to literally get sick and sometimes be in bed for up to three days after encountering crowds. They seemed to zap my energy and I would be filled with all the negative emotions they carried. Many times I would just cry uncontrollably, not understanding for whom I wept.

This forced me to study long and hard to find answers to what was happening to me. Spirit led me to the perfect books and spiritual teachers that began to remove my fear of the unknown and replace it with a deeper understanding of what I was going through. I was set on a beautiful journey. One that would lead me to many wonderful paths and to writing this book, which I was told I would do many years ago.

In this book, I will share some of the lessons that were given to me from Spirit. Without these lessons,

I don't know where I would be, because there was no one there for me to talk to. If I had told anyone what was happening to me, they would not have understood. They probably would have thought I was crazy. I wasn't far from thinking the same thing myself. I could confide in no one. Spirit was the only counsel I had. When it was convenient and necessary, they would guide me to a new book or teacher. It was always a way of reinforcing the lessons they had previously given me and also a way to bestow new wisdom upon me. Whatever I learned, I eagerly put it into practice, first by applying the knowledge to my own life and then by sharing it with others.

Little did I know that this was a foreign concept to most, communicating with an "inner voice." For me, it was as natural as having a shadow. It was with me all the time and I always knew that I was never alone. It is my best friend, my comforter, my loving guide, and my personal guru. It took me a while to accept that everyone didn't have this awesome companion. Well, I should say that they weren't aware of it, because we all have access to this. The ability to communicate with this inner voice has to be developed. The more you listen, the stronger it gets.

Because of this inner voice, which I lovingly call Spirit, my life has been one of conscious living and learning. I am always aware that I am learning valuable lessons, no matter how they appear. In fact,

I have found the more painful the experience, the greater the lesson. Spirit always made it clear to me that I was in a classroom. Every situation offers nuggets of wisdom that I came here to learn. I know that one of my tasks is to teach others about self-love and forgiveness. I am here to teach through my example. This idea makes me look at life in a way that most never do. I'm always looking for the lessons in every situation. Every day becomes an opportunity to grow and to learn something new. I'm becoming aware of how powerful I am, and how I create my world with my thoughts and intentions. We all do this, but most are simply not aware of it. The knowledge of this will make you a more conscious *Being.*

I have so much to share with you, and perhaps there are many books within me. But my desire in writing this book is to share a great deal of wisdom that Spirit has imparted to me, to help me get through my life. I'm sharing it in the hope that it will also assist you on your journey. I would not be the person I am without my loving Spirit that has guided me through my life. I have made an attempt to put into words lessons that I receive intuitively. All of my senses are engaged in this process. I can feel it, I see pictures, and I hear words. It's with an inner sight and inner hearing that these truths are revealed to me. I then have to find the perfect words to express the feelings or what I see. This process can be a long and tedious one as I write this book, because each word has to "feel" right or I must keep going over it until I find the right one.

I have been led to many teachers along my path and each one has been a source of confirmation for all that Spirit has shown me. Many of my teachers were not human; some were insects, birds, water mammals, squirrels, and even rabbits. It's really amazing how much we can learn about ourselves by observing our surroundings.

When you start on the path with Spirit, many wonders await you. You will be on a path of expansion and self-realization. You will learn many new things, things that you may not have thought about before. You will learn a new language, how to interpret the way you "feel." This may be the first time you thought of it this way, that "feeling" really is a language. It's a way of communicating non-verbally. Believe me, it's always an adventure when Spirit is your companion.

In this book you must remain open. It may be necessary to read one chapter at a time and then close the book and allow it to penetrate deeper. I have written this book in the way that Spirit teaches me. They give me many lessons through the use of metaphors, but they can also be quite frank and straight to the point. They rarely "sugar coat" anything, but they do have a wonderful sense of humor. In the first section, we are setting up the conditions that must be understood before going on. Everything else in this book is dependent on these chapters being understood, for they are the foundation on which this book is written. The second section gives you life examples and a new way of looking at them. The third and final section holds some powerful wisdom. If understood and put into practice, it will help you create the most wonderful life you could ever dream of. Don't skip through any of the chapters until you have read the entire book at least once, and when possible read out loud. Each chapter is like a step on a ladder; if you skip one, you might slip up and lose your footing. It may prevent you from being able to follow along. The chapters were written to be built upon. Take your time, don't rush through it. It is a book that is meant for you to apply to your life. Each chapter is meant to be a "mirror" for you, to allow you to gaze more deeply into your own material manifestations.

Because my teachers came from all walks of life, including the sciences, you will hear a correlation between quantum physics and spirituality, in the sense of how they both relate to energy and how we create our realities. You will hear the echo of many disembodied voices, including Abraham, Seth, and Solomon, with whom I have just recently become familiar. Their wisdom has been greatly appreciated by me, as these teachers are some of the only ones that mirrored the lessons of Spirit back to me in perfection. It makes sense that their messages should hold a familiar tone. Hearing them comforted me and made it clear that I was not crazy, but precise in my translation. I appreciate all those who have come before me. All the wonderful *Beings of Light* who took the time to write their messages down. They have laid a path of light, on which I walk today. They helped me find the *Light* within myself. And now, one of my deepest desires is to follow in their footsteps and create a path for someone else. May this book bless you in more ways than can be conceived and may the *Light of Source* fill you and comfort you on the journey to your *Awakening.*

Section
1

Understanding the Illusion

Doors of Light

The Awakening Has Begun

CHAPTER ONE

The First Manifestation

*"Humans feel powerless, because
they don't know who they are."*

SPIRIT

In order for you to understand your true power, as a *Spiritual Being* having a physical experience, you must know that you have chosen to manifest on this physical plane. Spirit said that our first manifestation as *Energetic Beings* moving into the material world is our bodies. To be more specific, the first thing we manifest is our heart. Spirit said, "You are your heart," and that you view your world through "the eyes of your heart." Keep this in mind.

The body is our cloak, our disguise, our vehicle, that allows us to participate on this physical plane. It is the form that we choose to take. The body is a crystallization of our most dominant thoughts. It is a perfect reflection of what we believe and how we feel about ourselves in every moment. It is the first place that we can focus our attention to see in the material world where our spirit is at the moment, in the Re-Awakening process, moving from the gross body to the more ethereal forms of our nature.

Your body mirrors your thought forms. Your overall health and wellbeing reflect your most dominant thoughts. The state of your spirit determines your health. Your attitude toward life is reflected in every cell of your body. When your spirit is experiencing a state of dis-ease, or lack of peace, the body reflects this. The body begins to show manifest signs of this imbalance. A very clear example of this can be seen in the human immune system. Negative thoughts immediately cause the immune system to weaken. This can be tested in real time – from thought to physical, immediate and measureable.

The next manifestation is your immediate surroundings: your home, your car, your finances, your yard, your bed, and so on. Is anything falling apart? Does anything need to be repaired? This is an extension of your energy. You have created this, and any signs of disrepair are a reflection of change or a need to attend to something inside yourself. Is clutter around you? If so, then you are holding on to things that you need to let go of, mentally, spiritually, and now physically. That which you can see helps you to "see" what you can't. This is a wonderful way to stay abreast of yourself on an energetic level. It's all you! When you begin to change energetically, the physical world around you will change too. It's beautiful to witness how it all plays out so perfectly.

When energy manifests into form, it disguises itself as something physical, be it a chair or a human. We then need special equipment to determine what this "thing" or "being" is made up of. You can't "see" energy, you only know it's there because of the measurements, and it's the reason for what you can see. Everything "seen" comes from the unseen, or quantum/energy field. The physical form is an illusion, playing out in the material world, because in truth, nothing is solid or physical. Everything is made up of energy, always in motion and ever changing.

All *Energy* is consciousness. The level of consciousness differs between manifested forms. This can be difficult to understand. When you acknowledge the fact that all energy is consciousness and that everything is made up of energy, then you must also accept the fact that everything on this physical plane has some level of consciousness. Even your blow dryer! That can be hard to believe.

Quantum physicists have proven that the quantum/energetic field is the source of everything we can see, touch, taste, smell, and hear. Nothing is static, everything is in motion, constantly fluctuating.

Energy is always being exchanged with the Field. We can't see this movement with our eyes, but on a molecular level this motion is clear. Everything we think is static is constantly blinking in and out of existence, even our bodies. It just happens too fast for our nervous system to catch. This has been proven, time and time again, with the most sensitive equipment. But long before the equipment was invented, the sages of old told us the same thing. Everything is *Energy* taking shape. The material world is an illusion, formed by energy.

All energy is *Source Energy*, and *Source* is pure consciousness. As humans, it is necessary for us to know that we are created from *Source Energy*. In order for us to be the powerful *Beings* that we truly are, we must acknowledge this truth. Understanding how we manifest our lives and what the manifestations tell us about ourselves is power. We are *Light Beings* made up of Pure Consciousness. Consciousness creates energy and energy creates worlds.

CHAPTER TWO

Life is a Psychic Event

*"You are manifesting your thoughts into form.
This is how you literally create you life."*

SPIRIT

The first time I heard the term *"Psychic Event"* was from Seth, the entity that Jane Roberts channeled. This was such a good way to describe what we call our "reality" that I use it often. It was one of the missing pieces that helped to describe what had previously been an enigma.

Spirit said to me that we need to be aware of how we create our lives in detail. Once we have this information, we can begin to put it into practice and transform our lives with it, creating more of what we want and less of what we don't want. The truth is that we are energy manifested into form and every moment we are in the creating process. If we know how to gauge where we are in that process, then we can have more control over what we create. Do you want to keep manifesting what you're manifesting or do you want to change something? Because as you focus your attention, so shall you create.

This is what Spirit gave to me to gauge where I am, at any moment, in the creating process:

1   *If you want to know what you're creating in this moment, check your emotions. Are you happy, sad, angry, etc.? You will manifest the like of this energy into form in your life.*

2   *Check your health to see what you have created, as a result of many moments of thinking. This is a manifestation of your most dominant thoughts, as it creates your body. (Positive, optimistic, healthy thoughts will improve your health while negative thinking will cause your health to decline.)*

3   *The present circumstances of your life are the accumulation of even more moments, that reflect your dominant thoughts and beliefs.*

Just being aware of how you feel in every moment can help you become more empowered and deliberate in the creating process. You have complete power over how you feel in every moment. And only you control what you choose to think about. You must take control of your thoughts and make a concerted effort to be happy, no matter what's going on around you. This is a master key to creating the life of your dreams, a life you really want to live.

Only you can control your perception. You have the power to see things any way you choose to see them. If something is not working out for you, then change the way you look at it. Or if necessary, remove yourself from the situation. Once you change the way you look at something, then you will change what you see. The way you perceive your life is the way your life will be. If you perceive yourself to be blessed, then your life will yield that reality to you.

You have a version of the world you live in, because no one perceives the world the same. In order for you to see what you're creating in your world, you need to look at the people and situations you are drawing into your life. Are you meeting wonderful people everywhere you go? Are you having positive interactions with people? Are you enjoying your life? Do things line up for you and fall into place with little or no effort? These things will tell you how you're doing in the creating process of *your* life experience, because you are creating them, consciously or unconsciously.

Positive thoughts draw positive circumstances and people into your life. Negative thinking draws negative people and circumstances into your life. Most people aren't aware of what they think about all day, because they allow their minds to wander. Many spend much of their time thinking about the past, and this allows past events to keep repeating, in the *now*. Same story, new people. Much of what people think about is due to unconscious programing. Watching television, reading the newspaper, chatting online, or talking on the phone allow us to be bombarded with other people's negativity. In order for you to take control of your thoughts, you must first take control of what you allow to enter into your mind. Remember, you do have more control than you are probably exercising at this time in your life. Be vigilant and guard your mind, only allowing your thoughts to focus on what brings you joy and gives you pleasure in every moment. This very well may be one of the hardest things you will ever do in your life, but it must be done. It must be done, in order for you to live the life that leads to true freedom. Freedom from fear, freedom from guilt, freedom from all the illusions that have held you in bondage. A life filled with the things that you really want: happiness, joy, love, abundance and so on. Taking control of your thoughts is a must, because your thoughts are creating your life experiences. Focus your attention on what you want, not on what you don't want.

Your life is a *Psychic Event* that plays out in this Time Space Reality. Your body is the primary manifestation for your *Energetic Being* to interact on this material plane. This means your health, finances, strength, clarity, and total wellbeing reflect the amount of *Allowing* you are doing on an energetic level at any moment. The *Allowing* is the tuning into who you really are. Permitting *Source Energy* to flow into your life and lining up with your true self. The events you create in your life will reflect how in tune you are with this flow.

CHAPTER THREE

The Door of Light

"Fear has enslaved most humans."

SPIRIT

Spirit said it is as though we are in a dark room, the size varies according to how much light we allow in. There is a door, only one door. The door doesn't shut all the way. There is a sliver of light that comes through the crack and because we live most of our lives in darkness, we fear this light.

Most people have been conditioned to believe that what lies beyond the door is evil. It is "The Bogeyman" in the closet or "Pandora's Box." We are taught that opening the door is to be avoided at all costs. That great evil lies on the other side. Most people live their lives in fear of the door and the light that splinters through it. They live their lives cowering in what seems to be a dark corner, fearing any greater opening in the door. They live a life of limitation, fear, and ignorance. They suffer needlessly in every way, as this is the manifestation of the fear that has gripped their lives so deeply.

The door represents the opening to *Source Energy.* It allows light to flow into our lives. *Source Energy* is our *Life Force.* The door never closes all the way, because *Source* is always flowing to us. We just pinch it off most of the time.

Those who dare to defy the conditioning of fear, and begin to open the door, are the *Seekers.* They want more answers in life and aren't satisfied with living in a constant state of fear. They are branded by the world as "weirdos," "hippies," "crazy," and so on. It is an attempt to silence them before they can share with others what they have learned. The knowledge which would free them.

Asking the question Why? Will lead to many things and one will lead to opening the door a little wider. The light that flows through the door will either scare or intrigue you. When you have lived your life in darkness, the light can be scary at first. Some are so frightened by the light that they try to push the door closed even more, creating blocks and barriers to limit the light that flows through. It is an attempt to protect themselves from the unknown.

The closing of the door is symbolic of living in fear. It manifests as sickness, poverty, disease, and death. Living in fear causes the *Psychic Event* that plays out as these physical manifestations, and represents the lack of *Source Energy* that is flowing through our lives at any moment.

At this point in the human Re-Awakening process, we are in a state of resistance. We, as a planet of beings, are not permitting *Source Energy* to flow through us. It is because of the resistance that the *Awakening* process is being slowed down. As *Spiritual Beings*, we cannot move forward in a state of resistance. We can only learn from the lessons of contrast that are being created through the resistance, but the movement toward our eternal nature is being stifled. If we could just learn to *Allow Source Energy* to flow through us, life on Earth would be much sweeter and more enjoyable for everyone.

Once you understand that the material world is an illusion and nothing is really "out there," and that it's all a reflection of what you have projected from within, accept the fact that everything is energy and that you are the creator of your own reality, then, and only then, will you see that you were never in a room of darkness. In fact, the *Light* (wisdom, understanding, truth, etc.) will illuminate your life and you will see that there were never any walls holding you back. Everything you thought was real begins to take on a new meaning. Once you accept that everything is consciousness taking shape in various forms, you will never look at your world the same again. When you gain the courage to open the forbidden *Door of Light*, you will see that it's all an illusion, and you will access your power over creating your life once again. Everything is the creation of mind, thoughts taking form. This awareness starts you on a path of self-discovery. It is the *Awakening* process, which I prefer to call the Re-Awakening, because we really know all this stuff. We only need to be reminded of it.

CHAPTER FOUR

Peering Into The Illusion

"Nothing is what it appears to be."

A QUANTUM PHYSICIST

At this point, it is clear that nothing is what it appears to be. Everything physical is made up of "non-physical stuff." Your five senses allow you to participate in the illusion of life. Without them, you would not be able to interpret vibrational patterns and determine everything to be solid or real. Your five senses are a necessary part of the world of illusion; they help create texture, color, smells, sounds, and flavor.

This need to believe in a physical world is paramount to our spiritual growth. There would be no challenge if we were born knowing that everything was an illusion. The challenge is in "cracking the code," it's in finding out that the world we believe exists "out there" is really a manifestation of our vibrational imagination. It is a collection of information that has been agreed upon by the majority and is not static or unchangeable. It's only energy that has taken form and appears to be solid. In each moment, it fluctuates, moving in and out of existence. It has the appearance of being solid because of our collective belief in its "realness."

Thought is energy and when energy is held constant, manifestations begin to take place. A manifestation is energy taking shape or form. It moves from a higher, faster frequency into a slower, more dense vibration, appearing to solidify on our physical plane of existence. This is basically the process that energy goes through to manifest in our world.

Why is there a need for the illusion and what lessons does it offer us? The illusion is a classroom. It allows us to create whatever we can imagine. We can manifest any situation or circumstance we desire, and in doing so, we learn great lessons from them.

None of us perceive the illusion of life the same way. We are unique *Beings* and our perspectives are also unique. We are shaped by our past experiences, our religious beliefs, cultural beliefs, education, environment, society, and social conditioning. And still none of us see the world the same, even if we have been exposed to the same environmental influences and conditioning. Our perspectives will always be unique.

Our conditioning starts as soon as we are born. We are taught that the only things that are real are the things you can see, touch, taste, smell, or hear. And in some cases we are taught that if you can't touch it, it can't be tested and can be considered a figment of your imagination, if no one else can confirm it. In essence, it must be agreed upon by the majority to be considered real.

I always find this part interesting, because on one hand your eye-witness testimony can send someone to the electric chair, but on the other hand, if you say you saw an eight foot hairy beast walking through the woods in broad daylight, then you're nuts! That's where the social conditioning takes place. Some things are approved of and others are not. If it's not socially acceptable to believe in something, then it becomes "taboo." No wonder we're so messed up! We've been taught not to trust our own experiences, when in truth, that's the *only* kind there are.

In essence, we are being taught limiting beliefs from day one. And the most dangerous of these are the ones that make us discount our own powerful experiences and call them coincidences or flukes. There is no such thing as coincidence. Everything you experience has meaning. There is something in it for you, something that only you can get out of it. No matter how many people experience the same thing, there is a different message for everyone.

Learning how to find the meaning that you're supposed to get out of a situation or event is a key to *growing* your spirit. Look at everything in life as a curious child. Not only do children seem to make an exciting game out of everything, but they can find joy in the smallest of things. A child would be amazed to watch a butterfly leap from flower to flower. Seeing this would simultaneously cause them to leap and dance, as if they were a butterfly, desiring the *oneness* with the butterfly, wanting to know what it must be like to be one. Our mission becomes to know that we are the butterfly. We have manifested it and it is sharing a very deep message of transformation and beauty with us. We must apply these lessons to our lives in order to grow spiritually. The butterfly is energy that has taken shape, it is a vibrational match to where we are at the moment and has been called into our awareness to give us a message. It has become a part of the *Psychic Event* that we have created on a vibrational level. Translating what we see in our environment, and knowing how it applies to our lives, is just one example of "cracking the code."

Learning Another Kind of Language

Translating vibrations is likened to learning another language. In fact, it is a universal language. There are various forms of translations. You can interpret someone's body language or feel the energy in a room that you just walked into. You are translating vibrations whether you know it or not all the time. We're so good at it that it has become unconscious. It's like learning a second language: when you have spoken it for so long you don't have to think about interpreting, it becomes automatic. We are now on automatic and use our vibrational translators without knowing it. And even though we have become quite adept at using five of our senses, we are limited, because we have access to many more. We are missing out on so much because we don't know how to access the other translators that interpret other kinds of vibrational information that surround us every day. We need to learn how to develop our other "senses" or vibrational translators in order to access this information.

The world, that appears to be solid, is made up of vibrational patterns. Our five senses interpret these patterns and from this we get colors, textures, flavors, sounds, and fragrances. You have more translators, outside of these five. For example, your skin and hair translate vibration. They are a part of your nervous system. They receive information and translate it into a feeling or a "knowing," and if you're more in tune with these translators, you can receive images or other information just like when you use your five senses. It's one of the reasons why Native American trackers keep their hair long. They are more in tune with their surroundings because of it. Why do you think the hairs on your arms stand up or why you get chills or goose bumps? These are indicators that something more than what your five senses are able to pick up is happening. These translators could be warning you of impending danger or that some deeper energy is passing through you at the time. Sometimes the message is received on an unconscious level, and it will take time to "download" for you to understand it.

You are a *Vibrational Being*, composed of vibrational patterns, just like the world around you. Each and every cell of your body is vibrating at a certain rate and, when you are healthy, your cells vibrate together harmoniously. But when you are in a state of dis-ease or imbalance, they do not. When you're out of balance, your vibrational patterns are out of sync and your health will reflect this. If this vibrational imbalance continues for too long, it will manifest into something physical and you will be able to see it. It becomes what we call a "manifest" dis-ease.

Your health is very important. It is necessary for you to be a healthy, strong, vibrating *Being* to have access to your other senses. When we realize that our health is a manifestation of thought patterns that have been held for long periods of time, we also realize that it is crucial for us to only think thoughts that are going to serve us. Thought is energy and at this point we know that everything is energy. Thought is vibrating at a certain frequency and it will draw the same kind of energy to it. So eventually, the thought will manifest into form and become something. Don't you want that manifestation to be the best it can be? That takes a conscious awareness of what you're thinking about. It's important! Over time it will manifest in one form or another.

The point here is you will be limited in being able to access your other senses if you are in a state of imbalance. It is paramount to be healthy, mentally, in order to have good physical health. Because it all starts as a thought. The stronger and more balanced you are, the more you have access to the other translators that you possess. The other translators access higher vibrational frequencies. They operate on a different level of awareness. These vibrations are less dense and need a more finely tuned translator in order to be interpreted.

We are so powerful as *Vibrational Beings* that we can translate a multitude of patterns simultaneously. We are not the limited human beings that we think we are. We are more powerful than all the super heroes you can put together. We do have super powers, but we have not been taught how to access them. The instructions on how to access this information is encoded in our DNA. The DNA is made up of light. It operates on a higher frequency. This information can only be accessed by a fine-tuned light. It needs to be unlocked by a different kind of frequency, one that we are not used to transmitting.

The Ancient Egyptians said that we have 360 senses. If that is true, then we have been existing on survival mode for far too long. We've only been accessing five of the 360! It becomes an understatement to say that we have been blind, deaf, and dumb, and didn't even know it. On a positive note, we have so much to learn. It's exciting to think of what lies ahead. There is so much to discover about ourselves. To my understanding, the only time we have access to these other senses is through a higher state of *Consciousness*. We have to become higher vibrating, more fine-tuned *Beings* to learn how to translate these higher frequencies. It really makes sense that this would be true. If we are all vibrations, then you would have to be a "vibrational match" to the frequency that you are trying to translate. You don't have access to something that you're not.

Section
2

Navigating Through Life

Doors
of
Light

The Awakening Has Begun

CHAPTER FIVE

You Must Choose to Awaken

"You are Spiritual Beings who have
forgotten who you are and
why you have come."

SPIRIT

Spirit said to me that we are on a journey, a journey through darkness to re-emerge into the light. We are all powerful *Beings*, who have chosen to take part in this journey. Some of us have become trapped by our own creations, and others have come to free those who are trapped.

Even though we are the creators of the circumstances that many have become enslaved by, the path to freedom lies within each individual. No one can be freed unless they choose to be. The laws that govern our universe decree that no one can be forced to *Awaken*. It must be of their own volition, a choice of free will. No matter how much you love someone or want them to be free from the illusions that have them trapped and bound, you cannot force the light upon them. They must "open the door" for themselves and seek the *Light*. You can only show them the way. The rest is up to them.

Each of us is on a journey to our *Awakening*. We must first free ourselves, and then help others to find their way to the *Light*. It is not a compulsory journey, the ability to choose lies with each person. The only influence you have over another's *Awakening* is your powerful example. The potential to influence another lies in the example of how joyfully you live your life. Allow your life to be such a joyous example that it will draw others to their own *Awakening*. The final choice to bring more light into their life will be their own. You can change no one but yourself, and this is most frustrating when dealing with loved ones and friends. But you must remember that the *Awakening* is a personal event. The path and the way it will unfold in each of our lives will be different. We must choose our own means to *Awaken*, knowing that all roads will eventually lead to the *Door of Light*.

Some desire to lead others with a strong hand to that which they call their salvation, when in truth, all paths will eventually lead to that one which will cause the journeyer to desire more joy in their life and to open their door a little wider. No one can stand in judgment from a human perspective. This is a limited view and it will be filled with false understandings. Everyone is creating the circumstances that they need to grow. And eventually all humanity will find their door and open it, if not now, in other lifetimes. For a large number it will take time and maybe even many more lifetimes before they will be willing to see the *Light*.

The darkness has caused many to live in confusion and has hardened their hearts. So deeply so that it is difficult for them to let go of their fears and false beliefs that bind them to a life of misery. These beliefs do not serve them, but they have been deeply ingrained in them over many years. There is great resistance in letting go of the conditioning, consciously and unconsciously. The battle to be free is waged within. Each person must overcome their own fears and be willing to let go of beliefs that no longer serve them in order to begin to see the *Light*.

It is the time to open your heart and your mind to a truth that resonates within your soul. You know it when you hear it, and you don't understand why. It feels familiar because this truth is in your heart and your soul is confirming it. This truth may shake the foundation of your world, challenging the beliefs that you have built your world around. It is scary, but in your heart you know it is time for a change. The knowledge comes to *free* you, to break the chains of illusion. A new path will be lit and you will be guided every step of the way. It's beautiful and at the same time scary, because you are moving into the unknown. But soon you will have all the confirmation you need for you to follow the path to your *Freedom*. Follow your heart to the *Light*, knowing that your heart will never lead you wrong. It's leading you to the door and soon you will have the courage to open it a bit wider.

One of the key ingredients to stimulate your *Awakening* is self-love. The *Awakening* starts within and that is where the *Light* begins to manifest first. It is through self-love that the *Light* will begin to grow and in time you will find yourself desiring more things that bring you joy. Your desire for happiness and a balanced life, spiritually, mentally, and physically, will be the magnet that will draw more of what you want into your life. Until one day, without even knowing it, your door will be open wider and your life will begin to transform into something amazing.

What is the *Awakening?*

When we refer to the *Awakening,* we are referring to a state of consciousness. It is a state where you begin to become aware of *All That Is* and your connection to it. You will no longer see yourself as a separate *Being* who has no attachment to the world around you. Instead you will see that you are connected to everything and everyone in some very deep way.

You will become aware of the power you possess to create your own life and life experiences through the faculty of your focused thought. You will see the connectedness in all things and understand "cause and effect." Fear will no longer prevent you from seeking out answers. You will have a desire to release old beliefs and patterns of behavior that no longer serve you. You will begin to see yourself through the "Eyes of Source" knowing that you are a wonderful creator and that you are a part of a glorious creation.

The *Awakening* can be compared to *Enlightenment*, it is a choice of words. There are many words that have similar meanings in our vocabulary, and this is what makes transferring a thought into words so difficult. Words can have different meanings for different people. But the essence of the thought being conveyed is the same; it's not always easy to put it into words. The *Awakening* is a state of *Being*: of Consciousness, of Enlightenment, of Awareness. All of these words say that it starts within: in the mind, in the heart, in the soul. It is an inner journey that will play out in our life. The way we create our life is through thought, and then the thought is transformed into a physical form. Hence, energy being equal to matter.

We cannot hide who we are from an *Awakened Being*. Who we are will be seen in time, because time is used in the manifestation process to reveal the unseen. Your life is a perfect reflection of your most dominant thoughts. One who is asleep or in darkness does not understand this concept. They believe that things "just happen" and that they can hide or put on garments to cover up who they really are. But in fact, there is no possible way to do this. To an *Awakened Being*, all is evident and clear. They understand the illusions of this physical world.

There is great benefit in the *Awakening*. It not only removes fear and limitation from your life, but it allows you to become aware of the creative process. This, in turn, is why you came – to be a deliberate creator and to create the life and experiences you desire. Through your *Awakening*, you become empowered. You are no longer a puppet in someone else's show, and you cannot be manipulated. You are in control of your life and you become a deliberate creator.

The *Awakening* can be initiated from many things. Whatever sparks this awareness quickly begins to change the way you think and see yourself in relation to the world around you. We will offer you some of the initial signs. Some things you will notice about yourself as you begin this journey. Since it is a journey of consciousness, you will begin to think and feel differently. You may not be consciously aware of why you feel what you're feeling, but it is a *knowing* that something is happening inside of you. You don't feel the same way about things anymore. And because life is a *Psychic Event*, you will begin to notice changes all around you. This description is not meant to be a hard and fast account of how it will be to embark on the path of *Awakening*, but it offers some general points to look for. Everyone's *Awakening* will be different, but there will be some signs that we will have in common. They will manifest to let you know that the process has begun. And the fact that you're reading this book could be considered a big one.

Here they are, and in no specific order. One of the first changes you will notice is that some of the things you once liked to do will become less interesting to you, including not wanting to be involved with negative people. You will have a desire to have more peace in your life, avoiding conversations that leave you feeling heavy or gloomy. You may have a strong urge to quit a job that you're not happy with, or discontinue a long-standing unhealthy relationship. You will find that many friendships will seem to "disappear" from your life without you having to initiate the separation. There will be a strong desire to read books or study spiritual things. You will have a greater desire to be in nature, to establish healthier eating habits, to start an exercise program or take yoga classes. You will desire to study meditation in some form or another. Whatever your new desires are, they will be strong. You will feel a strong urge to do it *now*. There may also be a strong desire for more sunlight, usually in your home or a need for you to get out of the office more and get some fresh air. Your choice of clothing may change, desiring different colors in your wardrobe. A need for brighter colors is a good sign of a vibrational shift. You don't have to change how you dress completely for this to be true. Subtle changes occur over time until you find yourself being drawn to different things altogether. An increase in self-esteem occurs as well. This will also increase over time. You start feeling better and better about yourself, knowing that good things are possible for you in your life. You feel like taking more chances, stepping out on faith, if you will. A desire to stop watching the news and less of a compulsion to watch television in general. You want more "alone" time to contemplate your new ideas. Less of a desire to participate in negative conversations or with social media platforms, realizing that it creates more drama in your life. Most of all, you desire to be happier and you are willing to do whatever it takes to accomplish this. Loving yourself and having more peace in your life become primary. You start realizing what's really important to you and you release the things that have been blocking you from your happiness. Again, this is a general overview. You will experience many things, not only in this way, but physically as well. You may begin to have experiences with the non-physical or experience your intuition getting stronger. Both of these things *will* eventually happen, but you will be ready for them when they do. What I want you to remember on this journey is to be gentle with yourself. *Allow* your *Awakening* to happen, don't try to force it. It will unfold in the best way for you. It takes time, and that really is the best way. Embrace it and don't be afraid of the changes.

*We want to offer some further explanations of what is meant by the use of our metaphors.

What is the *Light?*

When we refer to the *Inner Light* it represents *Life Force* or *Source Energy*. The *Light* in general, represents Divine Love, knowledge, wisdom, and understanding. It is Absolute Truth. It includes all Universal Laws, including the *Law of Attraction* and *Manifestation*. The *Light* will free your mind from bondage, the bondage that is created from false beliefs and conditioning. The *Light* represents Ultimate Freedom from all things including fear and ignorance.

What is the *Door of Light?*

The *Door of Light* symbolizes the channel by which you access the *Light*. It represents a veil, or physical apparatus that is used to separate two worlds.

By "opening your door" we are referring to you accessing a truth that will shift your consciousness and cause you to become aware of more. To gain an understanding that will forever change the way you view your existence and the world you live in.

CHAPTER SIX

Life is in a Constant State of Evolution

"Belief in Limitation is a sign of an unevolved state."

SPIRIT

Spirit said to me that energy is always evolving. The chaotic mess that we perceive the world to be in is only the manifestation of an unevolved state. Chaos will eventually become order. It is the natural process of things. The more ordered and coherent the energy, the higher the vibration.

All manifested energy is constantly evolving to become ordered. It is the most natural state. Once energy evolves to a high vibrational pattern, it becomes coherent. It resumes a state of pure potential, or non-limitation. It becomes one with *Source* again.

There are stages to our *Spiritual Evolutionary* process. It is a misunderstanding to think that because there appears to be chaos, something must be wrong. This is the way most people view the world. Looking for the things that appear to be wrong and making movies and television shows about them. The nightly news is completely based on finding stories that confirm the world is a mess and something needs to be done about it. Or just the opposite, they show stories that make you feel like there is nothing that can be done to change the mess the world is in. When you watch this or listen to it, it takes your power away and weighs you down with negative energy. A dose of this every day will surely keep you in a state of distress and a low vibrational pattern, creating resistance to your own spiritual development.

If we could see that chaos is part of the natural order in evolution, then we could focus our attention more deeply on the eventual evolved state that will come as a result of moving through this process. We would not make such a big deal of this stage of our development, as if this is all that it will ever be. Our focus and full attention would be on the end result, a more *Enlightened Being*. This would allow us to get through the process faster, finding ourselves in a higher vibrational state. But we continue, as humans, to stunt our growth by focusing on the chaotic state.

Through this attention, we slow down the process of our *Spiritual Evolution* as a whole.

Remember, we are talking about a *Spiritual Evolution* that the human family must go through to recognize our true nature and to become the powerful *Beings of Light* that we are in these physical bodies. It is the process of *Awakening* while still in a physical form.

When we stay in a negative frame of mind, it causes us to create more of what we don't want by our mere attention to it. As humans, we want to fight everything that we don't agree with, when in truth, we are fighting a natural process of growth that we must go through. It is as crazy as it would be to fight the chaotic stage of early pregnancy. When life is forming and developing in the womb, it mimics a diseased state. The cells are dividing at such a rapid rate that they imitate cancer cells. If we were not aware that this is the natural process in early pregnancy, and the process by which a fetus will develop, we might well mistake it to be a threat to the body and try to kill or prevent the process from continuing. In essence, this is what we do every day when we spend our energy fighting what appears to be chaos in our world. It is simply an unevolved state that must be allowed to develop and move through the natural process of *Spiritual Evolution* that will eventually yield a world of highly evolved *Beings*.

If allowed to complete the growth cycle, we would see the beauty that will eventually come from this chaotic spiritual state. It is only our belief in illusion and our ignorance that makes us prolong and retard the process of *Spiritual Evolution.*

Your Experiences Help You Evolve

There are no mistakes and you've made no wrong choices. It's all in the process of "becoming." Every choice you've made has helped you find more clarity to become more aware of what you want and to know what you don't want. It is only the perception that something has gone wrong or that you have made a mistake that makes you feel like you have failed in some way. You must learn to be patient with yourself. Don't be so harsh in your judgments of yourself or others. It's not always easy to see the bigger picture, because when we look at a situation, often we find ourselves smack in the middle of the details. This tends to create drama if we don't understand that no matter how bad it looks, it really is going to get better. But it can't get better if we continue to focus on how bad things appear to be. This focus keeps us stuck in a low vibrational pattern and brings more of what we don't want into our lives. Try to be optimistic, no matter how bad things appear to be. This will help to manifest a more desired outcome. It's something you have to practice and soon it will become your natural tendency, to be optimistic no matter what.

Each of us has chosen the best form to manifest in, to give us the experiences that we need and to help us grow on our spiritual journey. For example, if you wanted to know what it was like to give birth, you would have chosen to be a female instead of a male. This form would offer you the best opportunity to have the experience of childbirth. In the same way, we have chosen the best life that will help us meet our goal for being here. It is the best if we allow it to evolve. When we grow into the person that we desired to become, it will be clear why we attracted the life that we did, and all the circumstances leading up to that point will have helped us to manifest everything we needed to become the person that we chose to be.

We were given the unformed clay and given the challenge to form it into a masterpiece. Everything about us is perfect if we allow ourselves to evolve. We must first transform our minds, our bodies, and our lives, before our world will be transformed. The world is only a mirror of ourselves.

The individual journey or process takes on a larger perspective when everyone begins to self-develop. If each of us does the work and focuses on self-development or self-improvement, the world would change overnight because we are all parts of the greater whole. Once the parts are vibrating coherently, the whole will be also.

CHAPTER SEVEN

We all Have a Mountain

*"You came here for the challenge
and for the adventure."*

SPIRIT

One of my *Mountains* was raising my three children as a single/divorced parent. And the Everest of my life has been home schooling them for the past 23 years from start to finish.

There will be several *Mountains* you will face in your life. A *Mountain* represents great challenges that must be overcome in order for you to grow spiritually. This usually takes many years to accomplish. Once you have overcome a *Mountain*, you feel like there's nothing you can't do. It summons courage, bringing out characteristics of inner strength you never knew you had.

Your *Mountain* could be anything. It could be raising your children, a marriage, a sickness, an unfair prison sentence, or a million other things. The challenge that a *Mountain* presents in your life is there to strengthen you, not to break you. It isn't something you whiz through. It's something that brings you to your knees and makes you go deep within, to find the fortitude you need to make it through. It stimulates deep emotions, tries your faith, causes you to ask profound questions, and forces you to overcome your fears. These challenges manifest to help you grow spiritually.

Some people never overcome their *Mountains*. They become "broken" by them. They find the challenges too difficult, and instead of being strengthened by them they become their victims. We all know these kinds of people, and the best advice Spirit has given to me is to not become one of them. Remember, you have created all that you are living, even if you don't understand why something is happening. It's not happening "to you," it's happening "because of you."

This is always the most difficult part to accept, for those who are experiencing something painful, to believe that they have in some way brought this pain into their own lives. Again, I will remind you here that most of us do not create deliberately, but by default. Most are not aware of the continuous stream of thoughts that flood their consciousness on a daily basis. This is where it all begins, because thoughts eventually manifest into things.

The masses are creating by default, because of ignorance. But once you know that you have power over your thoughts, and therefore your creations, it becomes your personal responsibility to create more wisely. You must become aware of what you put your attention on and consciously shut off the negative programing that is incessant in the world around you. Choose your thoughts more carefully. Choose the conversations you involve yourself in. Learn to focus on good things, fun things, happy things. Just because something appears to be going wrong doesn't mean you have to call everyone you know and start talking about it. This is where we err. We propagate the things that we don't want and feed into them. It starts and stops with you. There is a difference between genuinely seeking out advice and feeding into negativity. You know the difference. Again, spend more time thinking about what you want or how you would like a situation to turn out. Avoid feeding into the negative. This only makes things worse.

"Count it all Joy" – words of wisdom to live by. If you can see your challenges as stepping stones that help to elevate you, then and only then are you seeing them as they were meant to be. The trials that life brings your way are there to help raise your vibration.

They're not in your way, they *are* the way. Challenges are present to help you grow mentally, emotionally, and spiritually. These experiences will make you stronger. How you perceive them is completely up to you. All experience is good, but again, you must perceive it that way. It takes practice to look for the positive in every situation that presents in your life. There is a lesson to be found in everything and that lesson will be different for everyone involved. Ask yourself why did I create this? And what good has come of it? This can be a difficult task as well, but the truth is that when you change the way you look at things, you change the things you see. Your perception creates your reality.

Your Spiritual Growth is similar to climbing a Mountain

When climbing a mountain you will experience biological changes once you reach certain altitudes. We do this spiritually as well. We reach plateaus in our spiritual growth that will cause our body to react in the same way as it would on an actual mountain climb. The climb up the mountain is a *Psychic Event.* It is a manifestation of what is going on within us on a spiritual level. So whether you physically climb a mountain or not, you will experience physiological changes that reflect the shifts in your vibration while on your spiritual ascent. Many people speak of their "ethereal" experiences they had while climbing a mountain. This is proof of a more profound reason for the actual climb.

Once you reach a higher vibration spiritually, you will need some time to adjust to the new frequency. The adjustment period will be different for everyone. This period gives you time to become acclimated to the higher frequency until it becomes "normal" for you. In order to increase your vibration you will need to become more tranquil and shed some resistance, more will be required with each step forward. Just as you must overcome fears as you climb a mountain, you must also overcome fear of the unknown when on your spiritual path. The true test of your strength and endurance comes after you reach a plateau. Here is where you will be challenged to maintain your new frequency for a certain length of time, until it becomes *your* constant vibration. Many people fall off here and return to their old frequency, which they find more comfortable and easier to sustain.

Spiritual growth, like mountain climbing, requires you to continue upward, raising your vibration degree by degree, in order to attain higher levels. At some point on your journey you will be challenged, and you must resist the temptation to cease your spiritual ascent. You must continue to strive upward toward your goal. The spiritual journey differs from the physical one, in that once you think you've reached the top, you find that there are more peaks above. There really is no end to your spiritual journey.

When climbing a physical mountain of tremendous height, the body goes through many physiological adjustments in response to the atmospheric changes. The thinning of the air can cause dizziness, nausea, shortness of breath, rapid heartbeat, tiredness, joint pain, stiffness, cold and flu symptoms, and more. At some point on your spiritual journey your body will begin to display some of these symptoms as well. If you are not aware that this is "normal" for most, then it will create some fear. Now, this is where many people will go to their doctor and the doctor won't be able to find anything wrong with them. Not understanding what's going on with your body can cause you much stress in your life experience. Many will want to ditch the idea of continuing on their spiritual path because of the fear that they may be harming themselves in some way. They don't understand that they are getting stronger and the body is only adjusting to the higher frequencies. The symptoms are in response to the vibrational changes that are taking place on a physiological basis. Most people never make the connection between their spiritual journey and the symptoms they are experiencing physically. The symptoms will come and go over a period of time. Some adjust to atmospheric changes more quickly than others, and the same will be true for acclimating to new vibrational frequencies. The more exposure you have to them, the faster you will adjust. Those who climb mountains on a regular basis, or who live in the immediate area, are unaffected by the atmospheric changes. Their bodies have adjusted to life on the mountain. The more you are exposed to higher frequencies, the less you will experience the symptoms. Your body will become accustomed to the higher frequency and it will become easier for you to remain there. It is important that you do not allow fear to paralyze or to inhibit your spiritual growth. You are encouraged to remain positive, carefree, and non-resistant on your spiritual journey for expansion.

If you have prepared yourself mentally for the attainment of higher frequencies, it will be easier for you to maintain them when they come. If not, you will find yourself feeling uncomfortable and fearful when you experience a new level. You will have a greater desire to return to a more comfortable frequency, one that you have grown accustomed to.

I will give you an example here. Someone has a desire to stop smoking. This will improve their health and definitely help to raise their vibrational frequency, but the desire alone will not be enough to make the switch. They need to establish a mental attitude that will give them the internal willpower to make it through the challenges that lie ahead.

If no mental atmosphere for change has been established within this person, after a few days or a few hours they will find it easier to return to a more comfortable vibration of the old pattern. They will begin smoking again. This is one of the plateaus that we spoke of earlier. It is a test of willpower and if the attempt for change fails, then they will have to face the challenge again before attaining a new frequency. The only difference between maintaining a new vibrational pattern and an old one is that you've become accustomed to the old one over time and it has become more comfortable for you. With greater intention and desire, it will become easier to maintain a new frequency the longer you hold it.

Your willpower and desire for change have to be strong, strong enough to help you maintain a new frequency. If you succeed in holding the new vibrational pattern for a long enough period of time, then it will become effortless for you to remain on your new path. Your desire for a new way of life has to be stronger than your inclination to continue the old way. It's always easier to keep doing what you've been doing, because you have become accustomed to it. That doesn't mean it's good for you, even though it's comfortable.

Growth requires change and letting go. In order to grow, you must be willing to give up something. And more often than not, that something is a thing you've become really comfortable with, whether it's a belief or something tangible. You must be willing to release it if it stands in the way of your spiritual ascension. Most people want change, but without having to give up anything. They want change to be easy, but change is only easy if you believe it is. Affirm it, speak it aloud until you believe it. You cannot conceive how powerful this is until you begin living it. The power is not in your words, it's in your belief of what you are saying. Remember, you consciously create your reality by directing your thoughts. Beliefs are just thoughts you keep thinking without resistance.

The wonderful thing about the *Mountain* is all the lessons you learn while climbing it. You must learn to have patience with yourself, to pace yourself through life. You must learn to trust your instincts, this will assist you greatly on your path. You must overcome your fears, whatever they may be. The *Mountain* has many valuable lessons to teach and remember you have asked for them all, because it's your *Mountain*, you created it.

CHAPTER EIGHT

Some People are Bridges

"Letting go is a key to your freedom."

SPIRIT

Our lives are filled with endless relationships. We are intertwined into the human family upon birth. In truth, our relationships are very much spiritual, but on this plane they play out as corporeal relationships in the form of family, friends, intimate relations, acquaintances, and strangers. We like to think that our reality is filled with these kinds of associations, that someone is a stranger upon meeting them for the first time. This of course is not true. No one is really a stranger, we are all part of a larger spiritual family that have decided to play out roles in each other's lives to help one another work through whatever it is that we desire to accomplish.

The greatest lessons that we will face will come through the relationships that we establish while on this physical plane. These associations comprise our life experiences while on Earth. We have other relations that were not acknowledged above. We do establish kinships with other entities including our animal family on this planet. These alliances are very important to our spiritual growth as well, but we will limit our discussion to our human affiliations in this chapter.

Because our lives are made up of *Psychic Events*, you can only guess that our relationships are some of the most profound manifestations. They are exact replicas of the relationship we are having with our self in every moment. They are mirror images of our inner atmosphere. They display all of the hidden, internal truths. You cannot deny the accuracy of what appears before you. If you want to know who you are, then just look around you. It is not possible for a person to be in your reality unless they are reflecting something inside of you.

Look at those closest to you. If these people are loving, kind, generous, devoted, and sincere, then that's who you are on the inside. They are a reflection of you. It can only be this way. If you are surrounded by greedy, selfish, angry, and unloving people, then you know you have some work to do. These people cannot be in your life unless they are reflecting something inside of you, even if in the smallest way. They are teachers. These teachers have the purpose of revealing parts of yourself to you that you may not want to look at. In truth, no one is "out there," they are all within you. Remember, the Universe will only manifest to you what is your like vibration. This is a truth that is so evident that it is overlooked and misunderstood by the greatest of our human minds. The obvious is often times the most invisible.

No one wants to admit that because they are surrounded by unhappy people, they must be unhappy in some way too. But if you are being honest with yourself, then you will have to agree that something uncanny is going on here. This is where the waters get a little murky.

It is a necessity that you understand the *Law of Attraction* that is playing out here. The fact that you may have people around you who try to take advantage of you or who are not sincere in their admiration of you does not mean that you are not a sincere or honest person. This could be the case, but these people can also manifest in your life because you do not feel loved or feel that others can truly admire you. Your belief in this will draw these kinds of people to you to confirm what you believe about yourself to be true.

This is why it is so important to love yourself first. To accept yourself for who you are and if there is something that you desire to change, then do it. But if all other relationships are based on the one you are having within yourself, then it is paramount that you have nothing but love and peace in your heart for yourself. Because the "mirror" of life will show you if this is true.

The *Law of Attraction* works in many ways and one of them is based on your beliefs. When you believe something to be true, it will become true for you. It is Law. When you hold strong beliefs, they are power packed with deep feelings and emotions. The vibration of feeling is the mover and shaker of our Universe. You create your most intimate relationships through the depth of your emotions. They are perfect reflections of how you feel about yourself. This is what we mean by saying they mirror the relationship you are having with yourself or within yourself.

Relationships manifest for many reasons; other than the fact that we have created them, they arrive at the perfect time and place for us to grow. I really want to speak about the relationships that change our lives the most. Our children, lovers, close friends, and our immediate family. Wow, there's really a lot going on here. Our lives are composed of a web of relationships that span our entire lifetime. And they all have purpose.

When we don't understand why someone is in our life and that they have a spiritual purpose for being there, then we can attribute beliefs to them that don't apply. For example: We can meet someone at a time in our life when we are facing many challenges. This person comes along and assists us in getting through that trial and helps us "clear the storm." We begin to care deeply for this person, thinking that we have established a relationship that will last a lifetime, when in truth that person only came along to help us get through that period in our life. They were not meant to remain on the "stage" forever. The reverse is also true. You can be that person who acts as a bridge for someone else in their time of need. But for now, let us view it from our own perspective of someone entering our life.

They had a short role, and the time for them to part has come. But because we don't understand the larger picture or the spiritual purpose for the relationship, we desire to hold on to them. What happens here is that the connection that we have with this person becomes taxed in some way. A tension begins to develop that causes disharmony between you. What's really happening is that we are trying to force a situation that is not meant to be. Time is up. That person was acting as a "bridge" in our life. They were there to help us reach the other side. To pass from one station in life to another. They were not meant to be a major part of our life, just a brief but powerful companion for a designated period of time. But because we do not always understand the purpose and reason for a relationship, it can cause us to make a mountain out of a molehill, and create a great challenge where there was no need for one. The lessons we gained from the challenge were valuable, but not necessary. Much grief could have been avoided by allowing the relationship to come to an end at an earlier time, letting them go with love and appreciation for all that they did in our life.

When you reach a road block on your life's journey, you are grateful to see a bridge ahead. Bridges help us get over to the other side. They help us connect from one place to another. We all love those who have built such wonderful structures, and we often marvel at their construction. The same is true for our physical friends that represent bridges in our lives. They can be as strong as the finest steel or as whimsical as the rope and plank that comprise some bridges. Either way, they are there when we need them and this is enough to draw our admiration and love. There is a saying in life, "Don't burn your bridges." And we all know what that means. We don't want to damage our relationships beyond repair, because we never know when we may need that person again.

I want to make something clear here, because as humans we tend to make things harder than need be. There are signs and you will know when a relationship has reached an impasse. It will be clear. Don't be hasty in your decision-making process. Allow the situation to reveal itself to you. There will be many signs. Don't impose your own desires upon it. Allow it to show you what it is meant to be. Understand that most of our relationships will be transitory, not lasting our entire lifetime. There are very few relationships that you will enjoy for your entire life and those are very, very special indeed. But for the majority, they will manifest in order for you to gain some insight or lessons that could only be achieved by having such a relationship with that particular individual. Our lives have seasons and so do our relationships.

One sign that you are trying to turn a bridge into a life path is that you will remain stagnant. Just think about it. If you were moving from one end of a bridge to the other, believing that you were progressing on your path, you would keep seeing the same things over and over. You must move from the bridge before the vantage point will change.

If you are trying to turn a relationship into more than it's supposed to be, then you will find yourself facing the same dilemmas over and over again. You will want to have more with that person, either to become a closer friend or in an intimate relationship, you may want to get married. And you will find that no matter what you do to try to make the relationship grow, the other person will not respond in the way that you would like them to. Either the friend never remembers your birthday, or ever calls you just to say hi, and the intimate relationship is at a standstill for a prolonged period of time. If your relationship is not growing and you are not being hasty, then you may have to consider that you are trying to make a lifelong companion out of someone who is supposed to only be around for a short time.

Some very good advice in this situation is to give it time. Remove yourself from the "stage" and allow the situation to reveal itself to you. Don't impose your beliefs on the relationship. Be open to all the possibilities. Be loving in your state of suspense. This will bring about a positive outcome no matter what. It may not be the one you want, but all-in-all it will be good.

One thing to remember at this stage is that there could be many variables at play here. You may be ready for something that the other person is not. They may be learning self-love and are not yet ready to accept that someone really loves them or wants to be their true friend. All relationships are co-creations and both parties must agree and desire the same thing. Sometimes giving people a little space will allow them to take inventory and, in so doing, realize how much they desire to have you in their life.

If not, you never have to worry about losing out on anything, not a friendship, a love, or a ton of money. If one avenue doesn't work out, then many other opportunities will present in your life to bring your desired goal into being. It is Law. Learn to expect the best in every situation. This attitude will allow you to create your desires with less resistance. It creates a belief that nothing but good can come to you. And when you believe it, so shall it be.

There are other types of bridges as well. The people who create bridges in our lives are not only close friends, family, or lovers, but strangers as well. People who really play a short role on your stage. They may only show up for a few minutes or a few short years. These are the people who connect you to something or someone that sometimes you didn't even know you were looking for. They are the ones through whom you met your soul mate, or who helped you find the perfect job or occupation, or even the perfect home. They were there right on time, to put you in touch with someone or something you didn't know existed. Sometimes we call these individuals *Angels*. We never really get to know these people, even if we are blessed to be their acquaintances for a short period of time. They come and go very quickly. Usually we have no problem understanding this type of relationship and we allow it to be whatever it is meant to be. In this way we do not create any negative backlash, because we allow the relationship to move through our experience with no resistance. And we receive all the good that was meant to be had from the interactions with this individual. This is how we must learn to "allow" in all of our relationships.

Your greatest joys and deepest sorrows will come from the relationships you create in this life. The rewards are many and the sorrows should be few when you have a greater understanding of your reason for *Being*. In time, you will be able to "Count it all Joy." It's when you feel joy no matter what's going on around you that you've begun to understand. Love those who have come into your life, if only for a season. They have answered your call and when the time comes for them to move on, allow them to move on. Bless them abundantly and have a light heart. When you learn how to let go of that which you love, and trust that everything happens for your highest good, that's when you will begin to experience a *Freedom* that you have never known.

CHAPTER NINE

The Intersection of Change

"Change is to be embraced."

SPIRIT

Our lives are filled with changes and how you view them will determine how smooth the transitions will be. They say that change is the only thing you can count on. It is inevitable. This presents a dilemma for most humans. The human species, for the most part, resists change. It is obviously a conditional state, as are all other states that promote spiritual growth. By this we mean that humans only accept change if they feel it is to their benefit. In truth, all change has a blessing within it. Without change there is no growth. Life would be stagnant and boring. Humans did not come here to exist in a state of biological suspense or spiritual stagnation. Everything in the Universe bears witness to this. Change is a necessary component of expansion and growth. Though not always welcome, it is vital to our survival and our *Spiritual Evolution* as a whole.

As humans we fear what we don't understand and that's just about everything, so that is evidence of the need for a greater comprehension. When we know why something is happening, it brings a more peaceful state to the mind, one where we can be open to the possibilities of growth and the benefits that lie within. There is much to be understood about the human experience. It is important to see the world continually from its vibrational origins and to keep in mind that everything is made up of energy. All matter is energy and all energy is governed by the laws of physics. Not Newtonian Physics, but Quantum Physics, a science that is just beginning to be understood. If we could acknowledge that we are mere babies in the larger scheme of things, and just beginning to rediscover the truths of our Universe, it would help us greatly in our exploration of the unknown. Arrogance has a way of blinding a person to what otherwise would be obvious. This is a manifestation of fear.

Spirit has shown me that when we are going through a major change in our lives, it is only a reflection of energy shifts that have already happened within. These shifts can be best understood by using the example of a large traffic intersection. The flow of energy resembles this type of movement. Spirit says that the energy we are shifts directions first, then we feel it ripple through our outer lives. Every change, no matter the degree, will be felt in our outer manifestation. All major change creates a considerable ripple that usually brings about a challenge before it manifests due to some form of negative expectation.

This is a good time to recall what we spoke about in the chapter on the *Mountain*. If you have already made the shift within, and now it's being felt outside of you, then you have reached a new plateau. Your vibrational state is different. The outer manifestation that comes in the form of a challenge is only an illusion, because you have *already* reached the goal within. You may not yet be able to see the manifestation of what you've attained vibrationally, but the arrival of the challenge signals that it's just around the corner.

This is not unlike giving birth on a vibrational level. The labor pains signal the arrival of something from the unseen world, and in a short period of time it will become manifest in the outer world. Your outer world must catch up with your inner world. Just like a baby in the womb, you feel it, but you can't see it or hold it until it is birthed onto the physical plane. The child could not be born if it was never conceived in the unseen world first. This is the same as your dreams and goals. All things must have a vibrational beginning. And with time, patience, and understanding of the process, they will then be "born" into your outer tangible experience. The physical is only a mirror of the vibrational.

In order for you to shift directions vibrationally, as in making a 90 degree turn in your car, you will have to slow your forward momentum before completing the turn. This will cause you to feel a slowing down in your outer life. Sometimes it feels as if everything has come to a standstill, but if you are able to flow into the new direction with little resistance this would be considered a smooth transition.

When changing directions, things can either go smoothly for you or become a time of great stress. When you are in alignment with the change, you will have a positive expectation for the outcome and a positive mental attitude surrounding it. This will allow the transition to be one filled with joy and excitement. Think of this one as a new baby coming into your life. Your life changes completely, a large shift indeed, but you've had time to pre-pave or prepare mentally for the task. Once the pain of labor is over, there is much joy and excitement around you. This represents a major vibrational shift in your life, but one that is embraced with optimism, which creates a joyful outcome.

This mental state is a matter of conditioning. Because others have done it before you and for the most part things have gone smoothly, it allows you to have a sense of peace about this kind of major transition. There are always exceptions to the rule, but for the most part people accept this major vibrational shift with positive expectancy. It has a large effect on the outcome. The ripple of a new baby is felt in every aspect of your outer life, immediately. This changes your life forever more. And it is a huge spiritual transformation, and the effects will be felt throughout your entire lifetime.

Now let's view a major vibrational transition from the mindset of impatience or fear. Again, at a major traffic intersection there is a lot going on. Energy is flowing in all directions around you. You must keep your wits about you and keep your desired destination in mind. At this pivotal point in your life, the increased energy can represent many choices, confusion, drama, or fear of the unknown. This is a time of great transformation. It can appear that everything is going wrong or falling apart right when it is really coming together for you. The important thing to remember at this time is to be still. Allow what appears to be a storm to pass you over and trust that your *Angels* and your unseen helpers have your back. If you feel that your life has come to a complete stop during this major shift, know that it is only an illusion. Instead, see it as a forecast of the "new" that is about to enter your life. The intersection is a major crossroad. It represents new beginnings for your life.

Be patient and understanding of the process, as this will help you pass through it with greater ease. You must keep your eye on the goal and remember that you have already done the work. That's why you are at this great intersection of change. Now your work is to trust that everything you need to complete this process is already in place. You must *Trust* and *Allow*. Once you pass through this phase you will be able to see more clearly. You will see how it all helped to clear a path for your new direction. Many obstacles will have been removed and a great sense of peace will overcome you. Your goal will be accomplished, even if not materialized yet, and a new beginning will ensue. The materialization is soon to follow.

Patience is needed when major life changes are upon you. Ignore what appears to be and follow your heart. Allow the peace of your mind to carry you through your days. If you get caught up in the illusion, it will cause you much stress and take away your peace. You must remember at this time not to give the illusion any power. This is the point when you realize that the challenge has only appeared because somewhere inside of you, you expected it to. Any attention to the illusion or the belief in its power to prevent you from reaching your goal will only yield you unwanted things. Look at these challenges as temporary stops or yields that signal the nearness of your desired destination. Your desired goal is nigh. Trusting your *Angels* at this time is crucial to making it through. Trust, patience, time and a positive expectation are the ingredients for a successful transition. Be grateful for making it to your destination, even if you may not have arrived yet. Sometimes it's right in front of you, just over the hill. Your spirit will tell you it's near. Trust what you feel.

CHAPTER TEN

The Perceived Contradiction

"You must learn to trust what you feel
and ignore what you see."

SPIRIT

The *Perceived Contradiction* is when you feel one thing and you see another. It's a sense of knowing that you have about a situation, but when you look out into the world it appears to be just the opposite of what you feel. This is definitely the stage when you need to be patient and trust your intuition. Know that things are changing for the better, no matter what they appear to be at the moment.

This stage comes as you are traversing your *Highway of Change,* as you go through periods of spiritual growth in your quest for higher vibrational levels. The *Perceived Contradiction* becomes stronger at a specific point in your journey because you begin to think that you should be able to see your materialization by now. The important part is that you can feel it – the peace and joy that will accompany it when it arrives. This is a challenge, no doubt about it. The challenge is in keeping the faith and keeping your eye on the goal, while everything around you is showing you something completely different. It's a time when positive affirmations and other spiritual tools will be of great help in making it through. You are forced to call on your inner strength and knowing. This is where you have no outer proof that you have succeeded in manifesting your desire. On the contrary, you are given every evidence that it has not happened yet and you can begin to lose faith in its eventual appearance. But here is where you must remember that there is a delay between the vibrational world and the physical world of manifestation. Spirit says that this is the point where the delay is felt most.

What you are seeing on the physical plane is the manifestation of old thoughts and beliefs. It is actually the past. By the time you can see anything, it has already happened vibrationally. We think that when we look out into the world we are seeing the present, but the present is only felt, not seen. By the time it is seen, it is old news. Remember the first two chapters in this book, review them again if necessary. There is a delay in the materialization of thought. If contemplated long enough, the thought will eventually manifest in your life. So you only see old thought patterns, once anything is visible.

If you are a person who has not developed your intuitive abilities, this chapter may not make sense to you. But if you continue to grow spiritually it will become very clear in a short period of time. For all those who are in touch with their "knowing" this will be an inspiration. You will know exactly what I'm talking about, especially if you use other spiritual tools to confirm the energy that surrounds a specific subject. Those tools will confirm what you are feeling, but not seeing, and that should give you a sense of peace about the subject. Stay focused on the feeling of the successful completion of your goal. Continue to plan what you will do or how it will be once the goal has been accomplished. Feel as if it has already come to pass and you are living in that moment.

Make a list of things you want to accomplish and see them as if they are already done. See yourself sitting on that new boat, or driving that beautiful new car. Whatever it is, see yourself enjoying it now. If it's a certain position you want, act as if you are already doing that job and begin looking into things you will need to know or acquire once you obtain that position. If you want to have a baby, plan for the baby. Research prenatal testing and available birthing options in your area. Just get into the role. It doesn't matter what it is. If you busy yourself with the preparation, by the time you look up, it will be there or at least a lot closer. Don't worry about it, instead begin preparing for it. If you submerge yourself in the expectation and continue feeling good about the arrival of what you want, it will only be a matter of time before it shows up. Know that you cannot fake how you feel. You must really feel good about what you want. Do whatever it takes to keep feeling good, until your desire arrives. Don't allow yourself to be fooled by the illusion of what is surrounding you, remember it's "old" vibrations. Your reality is an ever changing thing and it's always following your lead. Instead of creating your fears, start creating your dreams. Don't be afraid to claim the good that you want in your life. If you admit that your world is your own manifestation, then choose to manifest the things you really want.

It is important to keep in mind that in order for something new to come into your life, the old must fall away. Part of what you may experience during a vibrational shift is the crumbling of the old. Many times, just before your desires manifest, you will face much instability. Things may feel as though they are being turned upside down around you. Your life is in the midst of a great transition at this point, and upheavals of varying degrees may be experienced. Things around you will begin to break down and need to be replaced. Old friendships that you've outgrown will fade away. Your reality will reflect endings and new beginnings in every way. The greater the vibrational shift, the more the ripple is felt. Again, vibrational change will be reflected in all areas of your life.

This reflection is due to the fact that the old must be allowed to pass away before the new can enter. This is part of the contradiction we sometimes fear. We desire the new, but we don't want to let go of the old. This is when it can get challenging. If you are holding on to something that you must let go of, you delay the appearance of what you say you really want. You must be in harmony with your desires in every way. Learn to let go with love and appreciation and allow the new to take its place. Now, this may mean that you have to let go of a dead-end job before the dream career or opportunity can come your way. This is a time that tests your faith. The *Perceived Contradiction* may make you feel like your world is falling apart, but in reality, it's really coming together.

The physical world around you will change without effort when you learn to allow your outer life to catch up with the new vibrational version of yourself. The tangible world will respond to the new vibrational patterns that are molding and shaping it into form. If you can learn to let go, trust, and have faith in the process, the transition into the new pattern will be a miraculous event to behold. Everything you have ever wanted is waiting for you, if only you allow it to manifest into your life.

All Things Will Be Made New

In order for us to experience the new, we must be willing to let go of the old. That doesn't always mean that there has to be a total replacement of a person or a thing that's important to us. It just means that there are times when you must release old patterns of thought and beliefs you hold about a subject before the new version can take its place. For instance, if you are in a relationship, you don't necessarily have to let go of the person you love. Sometimes this could be true, but not always. There are times when the relationship you're already in will be "renewed." There may be a need to take a short break or time out for the renewal in order to allow yourself space to release old patterns of thought and become open to a new vibrational version of your relationship. What you want to keep in mind here is that all relationships are a mirror of the one you are having with yourself. You are not trying to change anyone, but yourself. The relationship will be made new because you have done the internal, vibrational work. If that person desires to join you on your new energetic level, they will have to do the same.

We are all on a journey of self-awareness. Your personal joy is the key to creating happiness in your life. There is great power in *Joy*. All your desires will follow. You've probably heard this before, and it's true. The world around you is a reflection of you! When you change your vibration, everything around you must change, or be removed, if it cannot match your new vibrational frequency. You will then draw other "vibrational matches" into your world; this includes people as well as material objects and situations. This is how *All Things Will Be Made New.*

There are periods of change that you will face when going through vibrational shifts. Instead of focusing on everything you have to let go of, or all the things that are moving out of your life, focus on the new. Focus on the fresh start and the new beginning. This will help you keep a positive mental attitude while in the midst of change. This is something you have to work at. It takes a lot of internal work, but the rewards are more than worth it. If you follow the guidance that Spirit has put forth in this book, your life will change for the better overnight. Your peace will be increased and you will begin to allow more joy into your life. This journey is a *Mountain*. You will work at it, but it really is what you came here to do. You will become a deliberate creator of your life and you will own your reality by following your bliss. Give yourself permission to receive all that you have dreamed of and allow yourself to let go of everything that is no longer needed.

Section
3

The Precious Keys to Life

CHAPTER ELEVEN

Allow Yourself to Receive

*"There is no one standing outside of you,
keeping the things you want from you.
It is only you who does not allow
yourself to have them."*

SPIRIT

The idea of not allowing yourself to have what you desire sounds unbelievable at first, but upon closer inspection, it is the only possible explanation, now that we are clear on the power that we hold to create our own reality. When Spirit first told me this, I immediately thought I must have misunderstood. I couldn't believe they were telling me that I was the only one preventing myself from having the things I wanted. Why would I do that to myself? This had to be a mistake, or at least I thought it was.

Obviously, I was not aware of what I was doing to prevent myself from having what I wanted. Over time, Spirit began to show me beliefs that keep us all from having the things that we want. One of them is feeling *unworthy*. Although we have a desire for something, it doesn't automatically mean that we believe that we are worthy of it. Many times we want the very things that we don't believe we can ever have or experience. Whether from being conditioned by society or having acquired a low self-esteem, the belief that you are not good enough for something or someone will keep you away from it. Remember, it doesn't matter what you say, what matters is how you feel. If you feel unworthy, for any reason, it is enough to keep you from having what you say you want.

Another belief is not feeling *deserving*. If you feel that you do not deserve to have something, you will not have it. Even if it walks up to you and jumps in your hands, you will let it go. Again, this is something you say you want, but when it comes to you, you do not accept it. You simply do not allow yourself to have it. Feeling worthy and deserving are necessary for you to experience the things you desire in your life. If you do not believe you can be, do, or have something you really want, when the opportunity comes your way you will not realize it. You simply will not see that it is exactly what you've been praying for. Most times, this is because we are looking for what we want in all the wrong places.

There is a level of non-resistance that you must first attain before being able to manifest your dreams with ease. Some of us try to force our dreams into reality by banging away at the physical world. It may be true that you can force things to happen in your life, but this is not the way we are supposed to create. For one thing, it takes a lot more energy and you will be far too tired to enjoy the fruit of your labor when it comes. When a materialization is forced, it usually takes your peace. It does not give you joy and you don't feel satisfied once you have it. It's something that you thought you wanted, but when you get it, you realize that it is not what you thought it would be. There were signs along the way, but you chose to ignore them. You forced your hand, and this is what we call "working from the outside in." It's trying to force something to manifest that has no vibrational foundation, and that's why it usually does not last very long.

When you learn how to *Allow*, your world will unfold effortlessly around you. You will have acquired the skill of manifesting through vibration, not through physical strain. Creating as a result of vibrational management is the path to creating with ease. In order to manifest your dreams in this way, you will have to release the need to be in control and work toward raising your vibration through the faculty of *Joy* and focused thought. In this way, your world will begin to reflect things that only bring you joy. Your spirit knows what will make you happy and it will begin to only bring those things into your life. This cannot happen unless you *Allow* it to. It is a journey that is accomplished in the mind and then actualized on the physical plane. You must learn to trust, trust *Source.*

We will go over some vital steps to assist you in this process. The importance of these steps cannot be stressed enough. The first will show you how to create a vibrational foundation of non-resistance in your life. The remaining steps will establish a necessary framework for manifestation. You must take the time to build a solid foundation of non-resistance. If this is not done, the other steps will be in vain. Your fears and doubts will undermine all that you try to create unless you get them under control by establishing a vibration that will not allow them to exist. The greatest enemy to acquiring all that you desire is your disbelief in your ability to attain it. You must overcome this in order to manifest your dreams and desires into your life.

This is a chapter that you can read every day to remind yourself how to *Allow* the good that you want in your life. The following steps will help you break the unconscious cycle of obstructing your dreams. They will help you to uproot the false beliefs that continue to prevent you from living your life freely. These steps will help you reconnect to *Source,* thereby giving you the energy of transformation and transmutation, to create the life of your dreams.

Step 1: *Allow the Energy of Source to Flow to and Through You*

In this section, we will discuss a meditation that Spirit gave to me. It is a powerful tool that will teach you how to reconnect yourself to *Source*. I was given the meditation at the end of 2011 and was told to do it every day. I began to call it the *Internal Light Meditatio*n. It eventually grew into the *Allowing Meditation*. When you start doing the *Internal Light Meditation,* over time you will begin to feel energy vibrate through you. At this point, it will become necessary to *Allow* the energy to flow to and through you. You will then have to focus more intensely on releasing any and all resistance during your meditation, because the energy flow will become stronger and stronger as time goes on. By performing this meditation daily, it will help you train yourself to become more non-resistant in your daily life. In time, you will feel the energy flow through you, even when you are not in a meditative state.

This section is only meant to be an introduction to the meditation, a way for you to get started. It will become necessary for me to go into greater detail at another time, but for now we will focus on getting started. Let me explain how this meditation is different from others and why it is important for us to perform.

Spirit said, because of our nearly complete disconnection from *Source,* we have grown weak mentally, spiritually, and physically. We are now as close to a physical death as we can be and still be considered alive, somewhat like zombies. Those among us who have learned to harness a modest measure of light within, have become known to us as our Saints, Masters, Yogis, and Wise Men, but even they have not completely discovered the truth of who we are or how powerful we are to become. It was not the time, until recently, for such knowledge to be rediscovered. They were given a glimpse into the greatness and the possibilities that we hold as human beings, but only a glimpse.

Spirit said that for the most part our meditations have taught us to bring light from the outside in, mostly through the Crown Chakra, and then to allow it to pass through our bodies via different means, depending on the school of thought. I was told that at one time this would have been sufficient and would have worked quite well, but because of our current condition, this process will only offer us as much light as a candle. Candlelight could appear to be a great amount of light when you have been surrounded by darkness, but Spirit says that there has been far too much damage done at this point and we need a full overhaul. Our vibrations have become very dense and our frequencies far from being *Source* like. We are not able to draw a high frequency of light to us in our current condition. In accordance with the *Law of Attraction*, we can only draw to us what we are, and that's not a very high vibration. At this point, it is necessary to repair the internal light structures first, thereby raising our frequency before being able to reconnect to the *Light of Source*. All light and everything in the Universe comes from *Source*, but this does not mean that everything is on the highest level of vibration. There are many frequencies of light, just as there are many species of trees. Variety is evident in our physical world. We are now in the process of reclaiming our ultimate vibration, that of *Source*. It is a process of transfiguration and transmutation to reacquire our true identity.

Spirit told me to think of myself as a living cell in the body. See this cell as though it were filled with light and then connected to all other cells by thousands of tiny strands of light. When cells are healthy and connected, the light travels through each one simultaneously, giving life energy to them all. With this energy the cell can regenerate, heal, multiply, be fed, and expand in consciousness, but once a cell becomes sick, the light strands begin to die off and shrivel up. The cell becomes isolated and loses most of its connections to the source of light. The connections that remain are broken fragments which light does not travel through completely. This may resemble nerve endings that have been severed. Many of the strands turn black and slimy, as well as the cell itself, because they are no longer receiving the vital life force that once flowed through them. There are stages to this deterioration process and the more the light is impaired in the strands, the worse the condition becomes, until the cell dies.

It has now become necessary for us to restructure our forms of meditation, because of this internal disconnection. Spirit says we resemble an old abandoned building. This building was once a magnificent structure and was neglected over time. The idea of bringing light into the building, by turning on the main power grid from the outside, would at most yield a few unsafe connections. Maybe one or two lights would be working, if at all. They said at this point it is necessary to "rewire" the building from the inside out. When you do the *Internal Light Meditation,* this is what is being accomplished. Your internal light structures are being re-established and restored to reconnect you firmly to *Source Energy* once again. If you do not take the time to re-establish the internal light connections, you will not experience the complete transfiguration that is available to you at this time.

There are many walking this Earth today by candlelight. They believe that it is the only source of light, because it is all the illumination they have ever known. But within your body dwells a greater light, an internal sun. Through this light you will be reconnected to *Source* fully. The light of this sun emanates from your thymus gland. This gland is found between your lungs and just above the heart. Spirit says, once you begin to activate your internal light, the thymus gland will become more active. It has many functions, they are not all known by our modern day scientists. This applies to all of your glands and your body as a whole. Most of your glands shrivel up and become smaller over time, because they are not being "turned on." There is great purpose for everything that is found in the body. The body holds great mysteries that will be made known to us through reactivating it. There is much to be discovered about ourselves and our unfathomable abilities.

Once you begin the *Internal Light Meditation*, your vibrational body will start the process of recreating and regenerating light filaments within the physical body. This is the process by which you will once again reconnect to the source of all light. It is paramount that your internal light structures be renewed and that you increase your consumption of fresh water at this time, because the energy that will pass through your body will absorb water from your muscles, just like electricity. The water acts as a conduit for the kinesthetic energy to rejuvenate your body, so you must begin to drink plenty of clean water to sustain this transformational process. We have already discussed some of the changes you will begin to see in the chapter on the *Mountain*. Your body is a mirror of your vibrational self, so that means these changes will also become detectable in your DNA. You will begin to evolve into what we were created to be, *Super Humans*. This can be a long process, but because of the time we live in, it will happen with greater speed. We have entered the *Dawn*, the time of the *Awakening*.

There are several ways to tap into this *Spiritual Evolution* that is taking place on our planet today. You can begin to meditate to reconnect yourself intentionally or just be near someone who has already begun the reconnection process. Others who have triggered their internal light connections can stimulate yours through their very presence. This book will also quicken your reconnection. We are all joined on a deeper vibrational level, and we can benefit from the growth of one another. There are many ways to start your regeneration of light connections, through your intentional actions, or by coming in contact with someone else. If you did not start the process through your own conscious intent, eventually you will have to continue deliberately. You will only reach the heights of transformation when you desire to do so. The *Internal Light Meditation* will help you speed up this process. Once one human has begun the light transformation, there is no way of stopping it.

We have been deficient in our connection to *Source Energy* for so long that we have no idea what it truly means to be alive. We are mere shadows of the great *Beings of Light* that we are in these bodies. As physical *Beings* we have been functioning on survival mode for centuries with very little life force passing through us. This unhealthy state is a manifestation of our vibrational imperfection. We have been cut off from *Source Energy* on the deepest levels and our physical condition is a reflection of this prolonged disconnection. We must learn to plug ourselves back into the flow of energy that pervades the air that surrounds us. This energy cannot be seen, only felt. It is *Source Energy*, from which all things are born. It surrounds us on every side, yet we never knew it was there until recently. It gives us life, and life more abundantly. It is what we are made of, what everything is made of. It is the source of all matter and therefore consciousness. It is very real, but it must be experienced in order for you to understand it. By tapping into *Source Energy* you will be restored to a healthier state, there is no end to this. You will experience more joy, more peace, and greater love for yourself and all *Beings*. You will begin to understand things that have been a mystery to you. You will have greater vitality, and you will laugh more. You will feel lighter and stronger. You will reverse the aging process, which is really a manifestation of resistance to the flow of *Source*. You will begin to understand why you are here and what you came to do. It's like having your memory restored as a light is turned on, and that's exactly what's happening. Your body will be rejuvenated and your spirit quickened.

This meditation will restore the internal light connections that have been severed. You will grow new ones. No one but you can do this. It has to be a voluntary task. You must desire it. Once you feel the energy flowing to and through you, you will then feel the ecstasy of being "home" again. This is a necessary step to renewing yourself spiritually and physically, to restoring your knowledge of self and to becoming the powerful *Being of Light* that you are. The journey is for us to remember while still in our physical bodies. We are already great *Spiritual Beings*, but we have come here to be interwoven into the physical world. We are here to master the world of matter and emotions, to become deliberate creators that learn through interactions with other *Beings*. We did not come to run from the human experience, but to embrace it. Our destiny is to reconnect the physical world to the spiritual. To reconnect our bodies consciously to *Source* and to experience the physical world through this connection.

The *Internal Light Meditation*

This meditation is simple. Be consistent and don't try to rush it. It took almost ten months for me to begin to experience the energy flow. Everyone will be different. It is necessary to have a peaceful mind and to let go of anything that is troubling you before you begin your meditation. You are striving for inner peace and the release of resistance.

To begin, you can do this in silence or play some soft music quietly. Lie on your back. Slightly raise your head and knees if that is more comfortable. The reason you want to lie as flat as possible is that you will be letting go of all resistance, and that is very difficult to do when you are sitting up. You will be given visualizations to help your mind stay focused and hopefully not fall asleep. If you do fall asleep, it's okay, as long as you have started the internal light process. It can actually help you increase the light, because when you sleep you are naturally non-resistant. So, if you do fall asleep while meditating, try to pick up where you left off when you wake up.

Take two or three deep cleansing breaths. Focus on releasing tension in your shoulders and neck. Now move your attention through each part of your body as you relax all of your muscles. Move from your head to your toes. You will initially feel the body become heavier. Just let the weight go, allow yourself to sink down into the bed or whatever you are lying on. Now begin to focus your attention on your heart. See the heart being filled with light. The light enters from the thymus gland. See the light growing more vibrant with each breath. *Allow* your heart to release and let go of any and all negative emotions. The light warms you and fills your heart with peace.

Now, see the light shine in your chest like a radiant sun, spreading out in all directions. Just stay here for a few moments, allowing the light to fill the entire chest. See the sunlight grow in size and in brilliance, filling each part of your body with healing energy. *Allow* the light to reach out in all directions and expand. Continue to see the light grow until your entire body is filled with brilliant white light. Feel the warmth and rejuvenating energies move through you. The light has now expanded all around you. You look like a brilliant sun. Continue to bask in the warmth and peace of this light. Just *Allow* yourself to stay here as long as you desire.

You can do this for ten minutes a day or more, but I guarantee you that over time your meditations will become longer. You will lose track of time because of the peace you will gain from the meditation. When you first start doing the *Internal Light Meditation* you may want to just focus on this stage of the meditation. As you feel yourself flowing more quickly through the steps, you will be ready to move on to rebuilding the strands of light. This next step will pick up where we left off above.

Rebuilding the Strands of *Light*

Now that you see yourself completely engulfed in radiant sunlight from within, you will begin to see strands or strings of light connecting you to everything in the room where you are. If you are outside, then you will be connected to everything that surrounds you. The strands look like an all-encompassing spider's web. There are thousands and thousands of strands that shimmer with the light that passes through them. You are at the center of this web. The strands move out from you and connect you to everything that surrounds you. As you continue to move through this part of the meditation, you will see yourself connected to the planet, every person, tree, bush, rock, house, building, car, everything, until your strands of light move through the entire Universe. As you do this, you will begin to feel the strands grow. Some will be thick and some thin. You will see them or feel them. Sometimes you will have the sensation of a spider's web on your skin, but when you go to brush it away, there will be nothing there and the feeling will remain.

After a certain length of time the *Internal Light Meditation* will begin to change the way animals and birds respond to you. This may take several months or longer. For me it was a little over a year before I noticed that seagulls were showing up daily during my morning meditations. I had never seen seagulls around my home before, but now they fly over my house every day. Squirrels and other animals will not be afraid of you, instead they will seem very curious. A squirrel showed up at my back door one day and she didn't want to leave. She just sat there looking through the door until I offered her a piece of bread, which she took and ate while sitting on my door mat. She comes by every now and then to visit.

The study of Animal Totems is a very intense subject and deserves more recognition. I will not go over it in detail in this book, but I would like to bring it to your attention. This subject gives spiritual meaning to the presence of animals and insects that are drawn into your awareness. In my case, the seagulls represent *Unlimited Freedom* and reflect my transformation. The physical reality around you will begin to mirror the vibrational changes that are happening inside of you. You will start connecting to all living things in a very different way. Now you will begin to know that everything is a manifestation of a vibrational nature, and you will learn to interpret the messages that are contained in them. You are in for a very exciting ride!

As you continue to meditate daily, the energy will become more intense. You will begin to feel it pass through your body while you sleep. At first, it may feel like an arm or a leg is losing circulation, a tingling sensation, then it will get stronger. The vibrations will move through your muscles. When you begin to feel this during your meditations, it is the time to remember to *Allow*. Release the tension and let the energy flow through you. Your muscles will twitch and jump, your eyelids will blink gently, or you may feel hot or cold sensations run through your body. Tears will flow down your face and your stomach will growl. It's okay, these are signs that the energy is flowing through you. Don't be afraid of it. This is when you may want to understand more about what's happening to you. Some people will experience strong vibrations and others will feel nothing. Even if you feel nothing, it is working. It is a most desirable experience, but it can be confusing. You may be exhausted by the experience at first, but in time this will pass and you will eventually have more energy and vitality because of it. Just stay positive and don't be afraid. Know that it is the *Light of Source* and you are beginning to reconnect in a very real way.

After Spirit gave me this meditation, within about nine and half months I began to be awakened by vibrations that moved through my body as I slept. It was always an hour or so before sunrise. This meditation made me more attuned to the sun and to nature in general. It is going to change your life and reawaken something deep inside of you. It is one of transmutation and transfiguration. It will help you grow and overcome all the things that keep you from realizing your true nature. It will help you face and remove the obstacles that keep you in a life of limitation. Your life will be filled with new experiences and you will have the opportunity to overcome your fears and release things that are no longer needed. Everything you let go of will be replaced with something better. You will find your inner peace and joy. This will eventually guide you to create the life of your dreams.

You have now entered the *School of Light*. You will become more aware of your dreams and this will become a time of great learning. According to Spirit, it has always been this way, but now you will be able to remember more of your lessons. This is a profound time in the history of mankind. It is the beginning of a new age that has never been seen before on Earth. We have grown from the experience of darkness. Every person who is ready to become who they were born to be will go through this "rewiring" process and become one of the greatest human beings ever to walk the Earth. This process cannot be stopped, the *Awakening* has already begun.

Step 2:   *Allow Yourself to Believe*

Belief is a powerful thing. Your ability to master the *Art of Manifestation* is connected to your capacity to *Believe*. Even in our current state we are able to do great things. Just think how powerful you will become once you reconnect to *Source*. This chapter is all about *Allowing* the things you want to manifest in your life. We've already laid a foundation for some beliefs that block you from receiving the things you say you want. Now let's look into what you need to do to help your dreams materialize. It is very important to know what your beliefs are, so that they do not conflict with your desires.

When faced with a challenging situation you must believe that you can make it through. You must believe in yourself, because you are the only one who holds the power to create your life. When performing the *Internal Light Meditation* you will begin to feel more confident in yourself. This will help you step out of your comfort zone and reach for things that you never thought you would. You will become a different person, the person you were born to be. Just knowing you have the power to create your every desire is life changing, but without the faculty of belief it is mere conjecture, because you will never realize it. You will never be able to create your dreams or desires without this most important element. Know that you can have everything you want. There is nothing too big for the Universe. You just have to believe and know that you can have it. You can't receive it until you believe it.

There is another step beyond belief and that is *Knowing. Knowing* takes belief to another threshold. It's where you stop thinking about what you want and just start expecting to see it. You know when you have reached this point, because you no longer have any doubt about the eventual appearance of what you desire. You simply "feel" it and begin to expect it. When you believe something, a vibrational shift takes place, but when you know it, there is no question about the certainty of its manifestation. The *Knowing* comes from deep within and does not waver. Once you attain this state, it will not be long before you will begin to see evidence of what you desire.

Step 3:   *Expect What You Want to Appear*

Expectation is said to determine the outcome. Spirit says that when you learn to expect what you want, you will have it. You intend it to be, without resistance. *Expectation* is a level of non-resistance that must be attained. You will not be able to reach this level if you have not learned to trust. No matter what, always expect the best in every situation. There is great power in your expectation. Don't be afraid to expect things to turn out the way you want them to, and remember to leave room for something better to take its place.

These are the steps to help you move your vibration into a place of *Receiving*, through first *Becoming* a vibrational match to your desires. You cannot manifest what you have not acquired on a vibrational level. If you can *Allow* yourself to reconnect to *Source*, and move from *Believing* to *Knowing*, the process will be easy and manifestations will begin to show up all around you. Practice makes perfect. Apply this awareness to every aspect of your life. The practice of *Allowing Source Energy* to flow to and through you must become a daily undertaking. The power of it grows over time and life gets better and better. The purpose of the merging of your non-physical self with your physical existence is to live through the *"Eyes of Source"* and to master the material world with the knowledge of the vibrational to make your life one with *Source Energy*, in every aspect. It doesn't matter what name you call this power – *Source, God, Brahma, Allah, Jehovah,* or a million other names. This power remains the same. It is *All That Is*.

CHAPTER TWELVE

Free Yourself

*"Know the truth and start living by it,
that's what will make you free."*

SPIRIT

We have all heard it said that you only need to know the truth in order for it to set you free. Just knowing something has never had the power to change anything. You must act on what you know before a change can come. Knowledge has potential power within it, but transformation only comes through its application.

The goal of this physical existence is to attain *Ultimate Freedom*, in every area of your life, because this is the only thing that will truly liberate you. When you achieve *Ultimate Freedom* you will acquire *Ultimate Wealth*, in all its forms. We will discuss the many different aspects of freedom that you can experience, but there is only one that will give you full autonomy over your life. You must strive for that form of freedom. When you experience lesser forms, you do not experience bliss. You can find contentment and even a level of joy, but bliss will continue to elude you.

The more *Spiritual Freedom* you experience, the more open and in tune you will be to the Universe. And the reverse is also true: the more open you are to the Universe, the more *Spiritual Freedom* you will experience. As we discussed in previous chapters, you must first cleanse the mind and body of toxins and negative thought forms in order for you to achieve higher states of health. This cleansing strengthens the connection to the spiritual part of you. When the mind and body are vibrating at higher frequencies, you have access to a key that unlocks the *Supreme Wisdom* that is within you. At this point you will begin to revive the other 355 senses that remain dormant. According to the Ancient Egyptians we have 360 senses, of which we currently use only five. Our great powers of manifestation and transformation reside at these higher frequencies. Once you reconnect to this level, you can start accessing the powerful and transformative abilities that you possess.

The knowledge of how to manifest your dreams into reality is hidden within you, along with many other abilities. In order to access this knowledge to transform your life and the world around you, you must intentionally *Free Yourself*. This has to be a conscious undertaking. The only way to begin the tedious task of conscious rehabilitation is one step at a time. You will be working from the inside out and the outside in, simultaneously. It will be necessary for you to be aware of your emotional state at all times. Learn to seek peace in every area of your life and strive to be positive in all situations. A positive mental attitude will open the way for the conscious journey toward experiencing greater *Joy* and *Freedom*. This alone will be challenging and will require you to take control of all outside stimuli. These outside influences can hinder your growth or help you find the inner keys to your path of freedom. Once you establish a healthier lifestyle and positive mental attitude, it will become easier to accomplish this.

Training yourself through the *Internal Light* and *Allowing Meditations* will help you attain higher frequencies more quickly and with less resistance. This will begin a sequence of powerful events that will cascade through your life. You will need to exercise patience during this growth period. You are performing a spiritual cleansing and it needs to be done gradually. Realistically, this will take many years of perseverance and commitment to the process before you will see the implications of your actions. You will accomplish great things over time. The spiritual detox will be mirrored in the physical world around you. There will be signs to let you know that you are cleansing and raising your vibration, and one of them will be a strong desire to clean up the environment around you. This includes your physical body. Your health and wellbeing will become of great interest to you; this will include your mental and spiritual health. At this point, in the physical mirror, you will see yourself cleaning out closets, basements, storage spaces, cabinets, garages and other places that are rarely cleaned, as well as ridding yourself of old acquaintances and bad habits. You begin to desire healthier lifestyle choices and nutritional foods that include herbal supplements, to assist you on your path to good health. Your total wellbeing becomes of great importance to you. Here is where you will also engage in some form of exercise to increase your stamina and flexibility. You are now witnessing the beginning of *Freeing Yourself* on many levels. This process will expand and grow deeper as you continue on your path.

Inside, a force will be growing. It will grow stronger year after year, as long as you continue to feed it. You cultivate your spirit by performing meditation daily, by thinking positive thoughts, eating healthy foods, and by exercising regularly. This list is a brief outline, but it will suffice to make a point. The evolutionary process is about finding balance between the physical and spiritual, both of which make up your *Being*. You should always strive for balance in your life. You are now fully aware that you are a *Spiritual Being* having a physical experience and you must fight the urge to forget that. You cannot get so caught up in the physical world that you forget who you are. Do not neglect the larger part of yourself, the spiritual-self, the higher-self, which is the essence of *Source*. The spirit is the unseen part of you that guides you through the darkness like a lighthouse. When you find balance between the spiritual and physical worlds within you, your life will reflect it. One of the first manifestations will be inner peace. You will begin to experience a profound peace and unspeakable joy, the kind that is spoken of in the ancient texts. Abundance in all its forms will begin to manifest all around you. This includes peace, joy, good health, friendships in all walks of life, wisdom, true love, and financial freedom just to name a few.

It is necessary for you to have full autonomy over your life in order for your spirit to be completely free. If you feel that you are under any form of constraint or limitation, it will hinder you from being liberated spiritually. Remember that belief in limitation is what creates it in your life. They, the belief and manifestation, are mirrors of one another. Many people think that having a certain amount of money will make them free, but this is not completely true. Money does not automatically equal freedom. There is an illusion present if you hold this belief. Money is energy and it is manifested in many different ways. The way in which you manifest your money will identify your current belief structure and your level of spiritual freedom. For example, if you are a person who believes that they have to work for someone else in order to make a good living, this will be true for you. And if you are a person who feels confined working for others and you must have your autonomy, you will become self-employed. Your finances will manifest according to what you believe. Our lives are complex and they mirror our beliefs in every moment. How we manifest our reality is an indication of where we are spiritually, in the evolutionary process.

In our society today, money is almost worshipped. There is no end to what some people will do to get it. What usually happens at a certain point is that they get the money, but happiness continues to elude them. Money does not equal happiness, but as long as you believe it does, you will never experience true freedom. It is time to let go of the false beliefs that have been cultivated in us, through television and movies, in order to sell us lots of "stuff." This is why it is such a let-down when you get what you thought would make you happy and you still are not happy. When all along what you were seeking can only be found within you. What we really want in life is to be happy and no amount of money or things will ever do that for us. Happiness will continue to elude us if we have not already cultivated it in our lives before we get the things. In the teachings of Abraham (Hicks) we are reminded of this constantly. Happiness is free, it is a state of mind. Everything that is truly important in life is free. We're just conditioned to believe that we need "stuff" to be happy. This sets us up for a life of disappointment and seeking material gain. We give our power away, because we look outside of ourselves for happiness. Most people spend their entire lives looking outside of themselves for that which can only be found within. Life is a mirror. Once you understand that, your battle of being ruled by illusions will be won. Then the work begins to develop that which is within you, and the art of mastering bringing it into form. That's what deliberate creation is all about.

There are various ways to create money and the way you bring it into your life will reflect the mindset you currently hold. The amount of money you draw to you will be tied to your self-worth and your ability to believe in abundance. The fact that someone has a lot of money compared to someone else does not automatically put them in a certain category. You cannot tell if someone is free or in bondage by how much money they have. Money can be acquired in large amounts and still create bondage. If the money does not offer freedom in all its forms, it is not true wealth.

People who have large sums of money can still have a poverty consciousness. I remember hearing Deepak Chopra say this over 20 years ago, and it confused me deeply. Now, after much personal growth and study, I understand what he was talking about. Spirit echoed this same statement to me in many of my lessons. Poverty has nothing to do with money. It is a manifestation of a certain mindset. It is a reflection of the spirit. This is why you can have millions of dollars and still be in poverty. It is a spiritual state that manifests in different forms. The man with millions of dollars may express his poverty by being stingy and constantly fretting over the possibility of losing his money. He believes that he is worthy of having it, but still fears losing it. People experiencing this form of poverty have a sense of being worthy of more and are self-empowered. They can have a stronger sense of freedom and therefore create it in their life. This is true of anyone with a certain level of financial wealth; they feel more liberated than the person who has very little money.

The person who lacks money, with a poverty consciousness, experiences poverty in a different way. The extreme lack of money is created through a low self-worth. They believe in limitation and do not believe in abundance. They feel disempowered and experience less freedom because of it. Remember, both examples are experiencing poverty, but in different forms. These beliefs are usually unconscious. They may not even be aware that they feel the way they do. Some form of conditioning is responsible for the unconscious beliefs.

Life is only a reflection of how you feel, in relation to yourself, in every manifestation. Beliefs make you feel a certain way, and thoughts create beliefs. Life unfolds according to the constant vibration that you emit, through your thought, into the outer environment. In order to truly *Free Yourself* you must "crack the code" of how to think, because your thoughts determine how you feel in every moment. The way you feel determines what you experience in your life and what you manifest. This includes your finances. In truth, wealth stands for much more than money. Wealth is as much a state of consciousness as everything else. It's important to understand that in order to experience wealth in its myriad forms, you must continue to grow spiritually. If you feel any limitation of freedom, it will manifest in your physical life in one form or another, either through lack of finances, lack of time, lack of peace, lack of good health, lack of joy, lack of personal freedom, or just plain lack in various areas of your life. These are all manifestations of *Spiritual Distress* in physical form.

The spirit is always striving to be *Free*. It must be nurtured and cultivated in order for it to grow in your life. This is the goal, to recognize your spirit and begin to develop it. A cultivation that will merge the spiritual with the physical realm. The ultimate marriage is forming a oneness between the spiritual and physical. It's what the Ancient Egyptians esteemed to be, one who mastered the physical and evolved the spiritual to become one, completely balanced. In attaining this oneness, they acquired great abilities. Once mastered, they became known to us throughout history as *Gods*.

CHAPTER THIRTEEN

The Journey is About Love

"Love Thyself."

SPIRIT

Love inspires us to see beauty and to create it in our lives. When our lives lack this powerful force, it manifests in many ways. It gives birth to darkness, we lack joy and our health begins to decline. We engage in self-destructive behaviors, feel empty, lack energy, lack movement, and our appetites become imbalanced. These are all indications of a distressed spiritual condition and a disconnection from *Source Energy*. *Source* is *Love* and *Love* is *Source*, they are one. It is *All That Is*, the only reality. *Love* is the highest and purest form of *Source Energy*.

Love is the energy that flows through the Universe, giving life to all things. It is the vitality that allows you to breathe, that runs through your veins, your muscles, and your nervous system. *Love* is what we need most. It is the life force that sustains our *Being* on every level. This is not to be confused with romantic love, because we cannot truly understand this phenomenon until we know *Love* in its absolute and highest vibrational form. We must embrace the pure energy that gives life to all creation. *Love* is what we need to truly be alive, to function at our highest, but we have never been taught its true identity. We have been taught to fear it, to reject it, not to trust it, and even to stop looking for it.

We are confused by this word, because we have come to know it through the eyes of a child. We don't have complete understanding of what it really means or what it really is. For many, the pain they have felt because of it makes them run away from it and leads them to push it out of their lives. They build walls around their heart, trying desperately to keep it out. Why have we been miseducated about *Love*? This miseducation has caused the human race to suffer greatly, dying slowly as one starved of much-needed nutrition. Most humans have closed themselves off from this life-giving force and are now walking around in a comatose state, getting just barely enough to survive on. We must realize that we ourselves are an unlimited supply of this powerful force. We are pure *Love*. We can produce this vibration in unlimited quantities, enough to heal the entire planet and its inhabitants of all the ills that plague us. We are a powerhouse of *Love*, but just as a giant who sleeps has no defense against the smallest of foe, we are powerless in our state of ignorance. We are the sleeping giants that are spoken of in the ancient texts.

Since there is really no one "out there" and life is a mirror of our relationship with the self, it is vital that you understand that *Love* begins with loving yourself, because it is all you. The walls erected around the heart only serve as a self-imposed prison. When *Love* is restricted and not allowed to flow, fear takes its place. Now this is where I want you to recall Chapter 3, *The Door of Light*. We spoke of the "room of darkness" and the fear that causes many to run from the light. If you recall, the sliver of light that penetrated through the crack in the door was *Source Energy*. This is *Love*. Understand that the more you cut yourself off from *Love,* the darker your experience will become, and the less light and joy you will have in your life. Due to the absence of *Love*, you will realize its counterpart and begin to live in fear. **Fear is an illusion created through a vibration that is devoid of *Love*,** just as darkness is the absence of light. Fear destroys *Love* and *Love* cannot exist when fear is present. In our delusional dark state, humans became paranoid. We began to believe that we were separate. This state of fear caused us to believe in separation from everything. We forgot that life is a mirror and that everything we see is only a reflection of our self.

Spirit told us in the first paragraph of Chapter 1 that we are our heart, and that it is the very first manifestation of our *Energetic Being* taking a physical form. When you accept that you are your heart and that you have been observing the world through the eyes of your heart, you will understand why you have perceived yourself to be in a "room of darkness." The darkness was created from the walls that were erected around the heart to keep out *Love*, to protect yourself from the *Light*. They were erected in an attempt to stop the pain that was attached to the experience of *Love*. As humans, we have only known *Love* as an emotional state or as a physical connection. *Love* in truth is much more than this. It is *Life* itself. You must come to know this force in its highest and purest form, and open your heart to the transformative energy that lies within it.

As a spirit, you were born into a fearful, dark world. On this physical plane, it is known as planet Earth. You chose to be born into this world, not to become dark, but to bring forth *Light*, to create *Love*. We came here to learn from our dark side and to be transformed by it. We desired to learn from this murkiness and to understand it from the perspective of our heart. This experience has given us great knowledge and has allowed our spirits to expand. This has been a transfiguration of the soul, a time of self-discovery, a *Journey About Love.* Now, the veil of darkness must be removed. We have learned that the darkest hallucination can be overcome when we allow *Love* to illuminate the way, when we reconnect to the *Light of Source.* When your heart is filled with fear, you shut out *Love*, you shut out *Light*. You view the world from the fearful perspective of someone trapped and bound by darkness. When you open your heart, you open your life to the *Light of Source.* You open to *Love*, and this is where the healing begins. Miracles become commonplace, because through the power of *Love*, all things are possible.

CHAPTER FOURTEEN

You Are The Door

*"You are the Gatekeepers,
holders of the sacred keys of life."*

SPIRIT

Spirit said that our thoughts create doorways into this world and into other dimensions. Each thought is potentially a new manifestation, bringing something tangible into our world. Thoughts are *magical*.

It is crucial to be aware of what you are thinking about, because you are in the act of creating. Something will be born from your thought if you continue to think it. Thought may be something intangible and you may not ever have considered how powerful it is to be able to think, but it is a potent force of consciousness that takes a physical form when focused over time. Thought, therefore, is dynamic and encompasses the true meaning of magic. It is the creative spark that gives life to energy, that holds the potential to become anything. Do not take your thoughts lightly. They are powerful creators, even if you do not realize that you are creating through them. You create that which you can see and that which you cannot. Some of your thoughts never manifest in this dimension, but are formed in others.

To all our moviemakers and writers, you have created "real" worlds through your imagination. Other strands of your consciousness are experiencing them at this time. The worlds you have begotten are as real as the one you currently abide in. Be mindful of what you conceive. Create more responsibly and imagine planes of existence on which you yourself would want to live. Manifest worlds of joy and happiness, because others are living in them. Just because you are not aware of this in your conscious state does not mean that it is not real somewhere else. It's time that we understand how powerful we are as *Creators*.

There is a great need for us to exert conscious control over our thoughts. This is a necessary and serious undertaking. The universe we live in is one based on *Attraction*. Whatever you think about, you get. If you think about all the things you don't want in your life, this is a sure way to attract them to you. Knowing this should be empowering, but some people find this to be intimidating. Becoming responsible for your thoughts should never be intimidating. Being a deliberate thinker is a powerful skill that takes time and practice to master. Use the *Law of Attraction* to your benefit, and think about what you want to experience in your life. You have the power to create it. Focus on how beautiful something or someone is. Focus on joyful, light, and fun things. Redirect your attention to situations or circumstances that please you. You will find that deliberate thinking is worth the effort it takes to do it.

There is no need to worry when you have a negative thought. You have a buffer of time to redirect your mind before the thought begins to draw like energy to it. You should practice redirecting your attention onto something more desirable each time a conflicting thought appears. Your mind must be trained to think positive and to be optimistic. The only reason why this is a difficult task is that we have been conditioned to think negatively and to be pessimistic. We are in the process of a *Conscious Rehabilitation* and you must be patient with yourself. You must have the desire to rehabilitate your thinking toward a more positive state, then the task won't be so difficult. The desire for change will help you focus your mind on more pleasant things and ideas. You must take control of all outside influences that intentionally bombard you with negativity, dread, and fear. Negative thoughts deplete your energy, weaken your immune system, cause disease, and cause your heart to beat incoherently – some very good reasons to avoid this type of thinking. Positive, happy, and loving thoughts restore balance and health. They strengthen the immune system, invigorate your energy field, and cause the heart to beat coherently, creating harmony throughout the body. This is why you want to think positive thoughts. If you are around negative people, you will feel drained and heavy. Remove all contrary people and circumstances from your life. Do not participate in gloomy conversations. Learn how to take a pessimistic conversation and turn it into a positive one. Avoid negativity over the internet and low vibrational television shows and movies. Turn off all outside stimuli that leave you feeling unhappy or discouraged. Take control of what you allow to enter your mind. This will be one of the most empowering things you will ever do. The mind is the most sacred of all spaces, for it is the birthplace of thought, and therefore the place where all life begins.

Your *Conscious Rehabilitation* will be a slow process, degree by degree. Be patient with yourself, there is much work being done on a vibrational level at this time. Your heart will guide you through this process, stay open and keep meditating. You will feel more empowered over time and your desire to be positive and joyful will increase. Soon you will find yourself being optimistic about things that would have sent you on a negative rant just months before.

You are changing, a metamorphosis is taking place within you. You will soon be able to see beauty and abundance where everyone else sees gloom and dearth. The first step in this process is to see beauty within yourself. No matter where you are today, you must start here, with yourself. You are a brilliant, awe-inspiring *Being of Light*, in flesh and blood. You have forgotten your greatness, and it is time to be reminded of how magnificent and powerful you are. You are a *Creator*.

You are courageous, strong, loving, and empowered with a gift that is all your own. You brought something special to this planet, something that no one else has. It is your gift to the world. Only you can deliver it, and it's time to deliver. It's time to *Free Yourself* from the limiting beliefs that you hold about yourself. It's time to shine, to bring forth your great powers of transformation, transmutation, and *Love* to first transform yourself, and then by doing so, the world. *Allow* your thoughts to create *Doorways of Light* that raise the vibration of the Earth. Never forget that each thought is *magical* and gives life. The time has come to release all beliefs that no longer serve you, and to start thinking higher vibrational thoughts, so you can begin to reconstruct yourself and your life on an energetic level. The vibrational reconstruction happens first and then you will see it manifest in your physical life. As you release negative thought patterns, they will be expelled from the body. These thought forms manifest as bacteria, viruses, and fungi, just to name a few. When you release them from the body, you will sometimes experience cold or flu symptoms. This is a cleansing effect. There are several other manifestations that you could experience as well as a result of your "mental detox." Be aware that everything is not what it appears to be. There is something deeper and more profound taking place within you. As you release old patterns, you will be healed on a vibrational level, then it will ripple into your outer world. Do not allow the inability to forgive someone to hinder your metamorphosis. Let go of deep hurts and memories that have kept you trapped and bound in a low vibratory pattern. They continue to keep you from experiencing the good that you desire in your life. You must forgive, in truth you are only forgiving yourself, and by doing so, you are choosing *Freedom*. If you follow this advice, you will be practicing higher vibrational patterns of thought that will give you life more abundantly.

Forgiving and letting go is never an easy process, but you must change the way you look at your life in order to heal. If you do not forgive, you only hold yourself in bondage to things that take your power and your joy. Do not allow yourself to be limited by any situation or circumstance, and be careful not to let go of one form of bondage just to take up another.

The truth will *Free* you. When you reconnect to *Source Energy*, you will feel an inner *Awakening* of joy, your spirit will begin to feel limitless, powerful, and most of all *Free*.

Our total existence is *magical*. We create our world by thinking it into being, but most never realize it. Our consciousness allows us to create countless dimensional *Doorways*, each thought having the potential to give birth to a new world. Our thoughts open portals into this world, and they are capable of creating greater joy and happiness in our lives. The quality of your thought is everything. Learn to practice how to be positive and light of heart. Do not hold onto painful memories or negative emotions, release them as quickly as they come. Learn to forgive, because you are only forgiving yourself. Be light of heart and forgiving, this will guarantee a life filled with joy, happiness, and good health. Let go of painful, heavy thoughts and replace them with loving, joyful ones, so that you can have a positive experience. This is vital to your health, because your body and life are literally made up of your thoughts. By thinking positive, high vibrational thoughts, you reconstruct your body to a higher frequency. Thoughts do not stay in your head, they are frequencies that are broadcasted to the ends of the universe, drawing the like of their vibrations back to you. See yourself as the *Powerful Being of Light* that you are, a *God*, if you will, the creator of your life events. The reason why life has lost its "magical-ness" is that you have forgotten that you are a *Magician*. You must become the *Magician* of your life once again, choosing wisely the creations and delving deeper into the mastery. Your thoughts create doorways, and so you need to be conscious of what you're thinking about all the time, because you are *Creating* in every moment. Your goal is to vibrate *Love* with every thought, only contemplating things that lift you up and bring joy into your life. The person who no longer lives in fear and negativity vibrates *Love*, and is already living in another dimension.

You are the *Savior* that you have been looking for, *Christ* is a *Consciousness*. You are *The Door of Light* that brings love and healing into this world of darkness. Now is the time for you to *Reconnect* to *Source,* to turn your *Inner Light* on. You must rid yourself of fear and the belief in separation in order to do this. Know that the higher you raise your vibration, the more you will separate yourself from low manifestations. Your high frequency will protect you while in this world of darkness. You do not have to fear, you are protected. The *Law of Attraction* tells us that we can only draw to us what is like in vibration. This is a built-in security system. Focus your attention on raising your resonance through thoughts of *Joy* and *Love,* seek after *Peace.* Everything else will flow to you from this same frequency.

Rid Yourself of the Belief in Separation

The belief in separation is rooted in fear. It must be removed from our consciousness in order for us to heal. Spirit said that the human family, as a whole, is suffering from an extreme case of Separation Anxiety. Upon further research, I found that they were correct once again. Spirit could not have used a better example to express the plight of humanity, because of being separated from *Source Energy* (but they also meant that we were sick because of our belief in separation, period). According to *PsychCentral,* this disorder is caused when children or adults are separated from their home or from those they love (*Source*). Here are some of the symptoms: fear, anxiety, social withdrawal, fear of bad things happening, fear of death and dying, paranoia (feeling eyes watching them, seeing people peering at them, scary creatures reaching for them), depression, difficulty concentrating, sadness, apathy, and more. This sounds like the nightly news, and what half the population of the United States is being treated for daily! There is a very real manifestation of what we call dis-ease in our modern day society. Drugs prescribed for depression, paranoia, and ADHD are some of the most prevalent, and antidepressants are the primary drug used for more than one out of every ten Americans from the ages of 18 to 44. Something is right in front of our faces and we just can't seem to see it. This is a major manifestation. It's time to look deeper into why we must let go of our belief in separation. Spirit said that societies that practice and believe in separation the most will suffer in their educational system and in the health of their population. Need I say more?

The belief in separation starts in the mind, then it becomes manifest in the body, the environment, and then the world at large. The root of this is fear, and it must be removed from the depth of our consciousness. Fear causes us to become paranoid and to feel threatened by "outsiders." When we perceive our lives through this consciousness, we create an entire world based on this illusion. Our modern day sciences and societies are perfect reflections of this belief. We have divided the world into pieces, calling it continents, countries, cities, townships, villages and so on. This is only a manifestation of the mental division of the body, a division that has rippled into our outer manifestation that we call the world. We see the body as parts, a heart, lungs, stomach, legs, eyes, ears, brain, and so on, and so we have created a world of fragmented parts, just as we have fragmented the body. When you believe in separation, you can only manifest it in the world around you. This consciousness must be reformed, the illusion must not be allowed to continue. The reality is that everything is one, there is no separation from anything, but because we believe it is, that belief has prevented us from seeing the oneness. Perception is everything, and it's based on belief.

Now, let's look at the body from the viewpoint of *Unity Consciousness*. The belief that the body is an extension of the heart begins to shift your perception. It is imperative that you see your body as an extension of your heart, there is no separation within it, you are literally your heart. When you hold this view of yourself, it will begin to manifest in your outer environment and then the world around you. We are not separate from our environment, it is an extension of our consciousness. When you rid yourself of separation consciousness and replace it with *Unity Consciousness*, your reality will shift. You will begin to *Awaken* to the truth of all things. Your life will become more synchronistic the stronger you grow in your new awareness. The synchronicity will be a reflection of the *coherence* that you have cultivated within yourself, thereby causing your heart and all the systems of your body to begin to function as one, a true state of harmony. This perception will start a deep healing on all levels.

The heart is *The First Manifestation* of your consciousness taking a physical form, and all the parts of your body are only extensions of it. It does not matter what we call them, in reality, they are all one. The heart is as continuous as the unbroken Earth, within the body, and you must see yourself this way, unbroken. The greatest and first illusion is fear and the second is separation. Rid yourself of these. When you alter your perception to see unity and continue to do the meditations that were given to you in Chapter 11, you will begin to restore the oneness within the mind and body. You will begin to feel the vibrations of your heart resonating through you. It will be *Reconnecting* to itself, through vibration, to all its extensions. This consciousness will cause you to experience a true state of *Homeostasis*, a perfect balance within the systems of the body and mind. *Coherence* must start within your consciousness, it is a perception, and then it will become a reality within your physical body. After that, it will ripple into your outer world, where you will begin to affect the society you live in. Once one of us reaches a state of *True Unity Consciousness*, it cannot be stopped. It will ripple through humanity, because we are as the cells in the body, connected as one, on the deepest of levels.

Every time you look into the face of another human being you should see a reflection of yourself, a reflection of *Source*. Restore the vibration of *Love* and *Unity Consciousness* in your life, this will arouse the *Supreme Wisdom* that lies dormant within you. This wisdom will teach you to heal yourself, and in turn, the world. Never allow yourself to forget that you are one with everything, every beast, every bird, every flower, and every butterfly, it is all you. Even I, I am a voice that calls out from within. I come to stir you from your deep sleep. My voice gently whispers, wake up, wake up, it is time to *Awaken*.

About the Author

Rev. Dr. Trenayce Talbert, DD has been an ordained Metaphysical Minister since 2001. She spent the first five years of her ministry exclusively focused on taking the message of Healing and Transformation to maximum and minimum security prisons for men. Since the age of 19, Trenayce has devoted her life to studying, practicing, and sharing the Art of Healing in its many forms. This includes an extensive knowledge of Herbology, Energetic & Intuitive Healing, and the Mind/Body Connection. She is the mother of three wonderful children, whom she home schooled from start to finish over a period of 23 years. While home schooling, Trenayce established a practice in Holistic Medicine. She is currently the owner of *Awaken The Healing Begins Now* and

Modern Belly Dance of Cleveland, a place where women of all ages can learn the power of healing that can be found through the ancient art of Belly Dance. Trenayce travels and speaks to women's groups on the need for Healing, Transformation, and Education.

Please direct all inquiries to:
questions@awakenthehealing.com

To book the author for a speaking engagement or to set up a consultation please contact:
Trenayce@awakenthehealing.com

Our mailing address is:
Awaken The Healing Begins Now
P.O. Box 27573
Cleveland, OH 44127

CPSIA information can be obtained
at www.ICGtesting.com
Printed in the USA
FFOW05n2025250815